A Hacker's Humiliations

A GLOSSARY OF GOLF GROTESQUERIES

A Hacker's Humiliations

A GLOSSARY OF GOLF GROTESQUERIES

Joel Zuckerman

Illustrated By Tom Matthews

SMG

SPORTS
MEDIA
GROUP

All inquiries should be addressed to:
Sports Media Group
An imprint of Ann Arbor Media Group
2500 S. State Street
Ann Arbor, MI 48104

Printed and bound in China.

11 10 09 08 07   1 2 3 4 5
ISBN-13: 978-1-58726-444-3
ISBN 10: 1-58726-444-7

Library of Congress Cataloging-in-Publication Data

Zuckerman, Joel.
  A hacker's humiliations : a glossary of golf grotesqueries / Joel Zuckerman ;
illustrated by Tom Matthews.
     p. cm.
  ISBN-13: 978-1-58726-444-3 (hardcover : alk. paper)
  ISBN-10: 1-58726-444-7 (hardcover)
  1. Golfers--Humor. 2. Golf--Anecdotes. I. Title.

GV967.Z83 2007
796.352--dc22
                              2007003239

Dedication

To the madcap miscreants of the Meeglemoon Cup, a hardy hacker band that has provided untold hours of amusement over the years, not to mention dozens upon dozens of humiliation episodes—enough to fill this book, and an additional volume besides.

In this bitterly contested yet convivial annual tournament, which rewards serendipity just slightly more than skill, the boys and I have all delivered countless shots of jaw-slackening mediocrity. These efforts make knees buckle, fillings ache, bladders leak, and eyes well with tears of hilarity or despair-ity, depending on which side of the golf ball you're standing on.

But for every two dozen wretched misfires, there might be a couple of Tour-quality (fine, at least crack-Am quality) missiles that home in on the intended target with stunning precision. We, like golf chops everywhere, live for those singular moments of exhilaration. For just a beat or two we masquerade as golf champions, freed for a delicious instant from the occupational bonds of making paint, making book and making airbags, peddling jewelry, alarm systems, plush toys, pizzas, tires, and substandard housing, litigating, banking, accounting, writing, and the like.

So on the tenth anniversary of this sordid affair, I pay tribute to Moon Cuppers past and present including Sandy Andy, Easy Ed, and Dizzy Izzy. Lou the Shoe, Nuge the Stooge, Mac the Knife, and Dan the Man(ic). Lurching Larry, Reload Richie, Captain Rivi, and Ivan the (Truly) Terrible. Dr. Feel-Good, my main man (servant) the Rookster, the Cable Guy, Jeff Novocain, Sattler the Battler, and "Howitzer" Hurwitz. And among this cavalcade of characters, including the Paper Tiger, the 50-year-old virgin, the Prozac Kid, and the Bearded Lady, one man stands above the rest. Lastly, inevitably, it's the cockamamie commissioner himself, the Man, the Marvel, the Moon.

For all you and your crew cannot do—this book's for you.

Golf is, in part, a game—but only in part. It is also in part a religion, a fever, a vice, a mirage, a frenzy, a fear, an abscess, a joy, a thrill, a pest, a disease, an uplift, a brooding, a melancholy, a dream of yesterday, and a hope for tomorrow.

—NEW YORK TRIBUNE (1916)

How the game torments the adventurous soul!

THE ARCHITECTURAL SIDE OF GOLF
BY H.N. WETHERED AND TOM SIMPSON (1929)

Contents

HACKER HALL OF FAME MOMENT
Mark Calcavecchia—Shanks for the Memories
at the '91 Ryder Cup

III—SHORT GAME SHENANIGANS

Introduction

At the 2005 Masters, Tiger Woods knocked an eagle putt off of the green and into a water hazard, incurring a penalty stroke. (See "On in Two, Off in Three," p. 110) A couple of years earlier, Jeff Maggert was leading the same tournament in the final round. He proceeded to thin a bunker shot that caromed off the lip and came right back at him, plunking him in the chest. (See "Rick O'Shea," p. 149.) Decades prior, Arnold Palmer was bunkered on Augusta National's 72nd hole, needing to get up and down for a victory, or two-putt for a play-off. Instead he lost the tournament by sculling the ball 30 feet over the green. (See "Bunker Blader," p. 90.) On the famed island green at TPC Sawgrass during the 1997 Players Championship, Davis Love III inadvertently dinked his ball sideways while making a practice putting stroke. (See "The Dink," p. 101.) John Daly once took four furious whacks in succession at a ball lodged between some rocks, drawing sparks, but not moving the ball a whit. (See "The Whiffer," p. 77.)

These household-name golf stars have won some two dozen Major championships between them. Their on-course prowess and off-course reputation have resulted in nearly a billion dollars of combined earnings. However, once in a great while, even the best of the best have to endure a hacker's humiliation, just like the rest of us.

The permutations are endless. We step to the first tee with 14 clubs, ready to play 18 holes, normally taking 80, 90, or 100+ shots. But the potential for embarrassment, the possibility of extreme degradation or mortification in any given situation, is infinite. You don't have to be a bona fide hacker to endure the never-ending humiliations that occur on the golf course. As noted above, these moments of extreme ineptitude happen to the crème de la crème as well. They just happen to happen to the likes of us a lot more often.

Misery Meter

THE MISERY METER EXPLAINED

Not all hacking is created equal. Some miscues are just mortifying, while certain duffs are actually debilitating. Some affect the psyche, while others make you sickly. Some hammer the head or hurt the heart, a few harm the ego, or injure the id. The Misery Meter is a subjective ranking of how the actual hacking affects the hacker both physiologically and psychologically. Make no mistake: All hacking hurts profoundly. The Meter just tells us how much, and where.

PSYCHIC PAIN

 I'm OK, You're OK

 I hear voices no one else can

 I answer those voices out loud

 Twitching has become part of the pre-shot routine

 I've discovered I'm illegitimate, adopted, and unwanted

PHYSICAL DISCOMFORT

A butterfly kiss

A static shock

A bee sting

A dog bite

A bus collision

HUMILIATION LEVEL

It can happen to anyone

A self-deprecating remark puts everyone at ease

Heart and head pounding, face beet red

The incident replays in the mind, like a dying man's life flashing before his eyes

Witness Protection Program, anyone?

INEPTITUDE QUOTIENT

We all make mistakes

Coordination was never a strong suit

Two left feet, two left hands

Tends to miss the mouth with the fork

Couldn't hit grain if he fell down a silo

SAM SNEAD
THE SLAMMER GETS HAMMERED AT THE '39 U.S. OPEN
PHILADELPHIA, PENNSYLVANIA—JUNE 10, 1939

In his first-ever appearance at the U.S. Open, two years earlier in 1937, sweet-swinging Sam Snead was the runner-up, finishing two shots back of Ralph Guldahl. He played the tournament 30 more times in the ensuing decades, and never could improve upon that inaugural finish. His quest was the epitome of "almost." The Slammer was doomed to a dozen top-ten finishes at our national championship, four times mired in second place. But the most galling loss of them all came early on, in 1939. History tells us he finished fifth, but never was he closer to capturing the one major title that eluded him.

He was leading down the stretch, but a bogey on the penultimate hole made him sweat a little. The fact was that a simple par on the final hole would secure the championship, but in those days there were no electronic scoreboards providing up-to-the-moment standings. The last was a less-than-intimidating par 5 of 558 yards, a hole that Snead would birdie more often than not. There was nearly a 30-minute delay while streaming fans were cleared from the fairway, and while Snead stewed, sweated, and fretted prior to his final tee shot, he didn't do the one thing he should've done: Ask the assemblage where he stood in relation to his nearest competitors.

Please remember that the paragraphs that follow, in which the protagonist (in this case a pro who became an agonist) was striving for a birdie 4, concerns one of the ten best golfers in history. It's not the play-by-play transcript of your Uncle Morty, a 33-handicapper at the local muni.

The drive was hooked into a bare, sandy lie, some 260 yards from the green. Attempting to get home in two, Snead sculled a 2-wood into a bunker, about 150 yards further down the fairway. Eschewing the sand wedge, he chose an 8-iron, trying to reach the green in regulation. Instead he slammed the ball into the face of the same bunker. His fourth shot traveled 40 yards into another bunker. It was here that he was finally apprised of the fact that an up-and-down would secure a next-day play-off. "Why didn't someone tell me that back on the tee so that I could have played it safe?" Snead snapped. No one answered him.

His fifth found the putting surface, albeit 40 feet away. His miracle effort to tie just barely slipped by the hole, and, half-blind with rage, he missed the three-foot comeback effort, finally holing out for an eight. "That night I was ready to go out with a gun and pay somebody to shoot me. It weighed on my mind so much that I dropped ten pounds, lost more hair, and even began to choke during practice rounds."

His failure to win the Open was a bitter pill for Snead, and an indelible black mark on an otherwise sterling résumé. There were two intriguing comments he made regarding his lifelong inability to capture ostensibly the most important prize in the game. He once said that if he had shot 69 in the last round of every U.S. Open in which he played, he would have won nine of them. And, addressing the '39 catastrophe specifically, he commented, "It was one of the biggest blow-ups in the history of golf. If I'd won that one like I should have, I think I'd have won seven or eight Opens."

Possibly true. But despite the fact that Sam Snead was famous for his off-color sense of humor, one can only (in keeping with the family-friendly nature of this volume) modify the necessary bawdy response and substitute a PG-version analogy that mirrors Snead's own Open wistfulness: If my aunt had a beard, she'd be my uncle.

Tee-Box Travails

Anna Banana

This sad sack does more slicing than the chef at Benihana. But strengthening the grip? Learning the inside-out "power path" to fire the tee ball down the fairway with a tight draw? Making a full shoulder turn so that titanium meets Top-Flite squarely, instead of dealing it a half-hearted glancing blow? All of those bona fide solutions necessitate far too much work on the driving range, or with the golf professional.

So, because Anna's ball flight looks like a boomerang, the way to bend the ball back toward the short grass in her addled little mind is to aim way, way left. The clock-face example makes this concept easily understood:

Assume the tee box is at 6:00. Confident golfers aim at 12:00. Power-faders might aim at 11:30; those who hit the draw might set up at 12:30 or even 1:00, and let the ball work back toward "high noon." But this gal is defeated from the outset. She attempts to start her ball at 10:00, in the sorriest cases even 9:30, and let it curve back toward the middle. Of course the ball gets exhausted by this circuitous route, and though it might very well end up on the fairway, it's usually so far from the green she needs binoculars to ascertain the color of the flag. And if this is the way she's consistently forced to play golf, then there's another clock-face element she should be aware of. Call it "quitting time."

Solution

By LPGA Hall of Famer Beth Daniel

I've been on the LPGA Tour for some 30 years, and have played in more than 500 Pro-Ams. So I'm quite familiar with Anna Banana and her sisters Hannah, Joanna, and Diana Banana. And I've met their male cousins, Bennie and Bobby Banana, far more often! Back in the day I was one of the longest drivers on Tour, my good drives always fell a bit to the left, so I know how to combat the slice.

The biggest problem I see is with alignment. Too many amateurs are open in their stance; right-handers have their left feet pulled back from the target line. This sets you up to slice. Your feet, shoulder, and hips need to be aligned directly down the target line. Swing down and through the target line, and don't pull the club down from the top with extra force. If you do, you're liable to open the clubface, promoting an outside-to-inside swing path, which will put slice rotation on the ball. Square the shoulders at impact, and you'll hit the ball squarely as well.

The Cart-Path Bounce

The unavoidable, inescapable cart-path bounce is the game's depraved way of adding insult to injury.

We are a nation of faders. All right, slicers. It's bad enough that our inability to generate an inside-out swing path in combination with our perpetually weak grips results in that pathetic glancing blow, devoid of power and chronically heading high and right. Our tee balls often cover 250 yards of airborne distance but usually land behind the pitch mark, barely 210 yards from the launching pad. Isn't it bad enough that we hackers are always the first to hit our approaches, wearing out the grips on the fairway woods and long irons that represent our only realistic chance of reaching that par-4 green in regulation? Must we also suffer the added indignity of having the ball carom off the cart path and head hard right into the brush, the forest, or somebody's backyard as well?

Everyone knows that sick feeling. You come off of a tee shot and the ball balloons, then starts drifting right. You make a series of rapid calculations as time stands still, attempting to vector the angle of descent, the position of the asphalt, and the wind currents as the ball hurtles earthward. A split second before impact you're resigned to your miserable fate, and to the

ugly smack to follow that scars both Strata and psyche concurrently.

Granted, we've all uncorked the occasional 300-yard drive when a mishit somehow manages to stay on the macadam, bouncing and rolling toward the green. Unfortunately this sporadic good fortune is dwarfed by the far more frequent occasions on which the ball careens sideways off the asphalt and into the underbrush.

Of course there are vagaries in the game, usually referred to here as "the rub of the green." But why must we deal with the rub of the concrete as well?

Solution

By PGA Professional Tad Sanders

It's amazing how misaligned golfers can become. They're thinking they are lined up straight down the middle of the fairway when they are actually aimed 45 degrees to the right of the intended target line, bringing water hazards, trees, bunkers, rough, and yes, even cart paths more into play. Inevitably the ball flies in a straight line toward the actual target instead of the intended target, followed by a comment like, "I can't believe the ball went so far off-line!"

Hitting the ball straighter starts with proper alignment. The leading edge of the clubface must be aimed perpendicular to the target line, and the body (feet, knees, hips, and shoulders) parallel to the target line. Try these two tips to help perfect your alignment:

On the driving range, take the time to place a club on the ground parallel to your target line, and make sure your body is lined up parallel to the club before swinging. This will help reinforce what proper alignment looks and feels like. And, while on the course itself, use an intermediate target 6 to 12 inches in front of your ball to help aim the clubface. It is much easier to aim at a spot a foot away instead of 100 to 250 yards away. Of course when you really do perfect your alignment, you may choose to aim for the cart path, particularly when an extra 40 or 50 yards might come in handy!

Dr. Double Cross

Definition: Treachery, betrayal, or swindling by acting in contradiction to a prior agreement.

There's water (or weeds, wasteland, wetlands, washrooms, wasp nests, whatever) to the left. Our semiskilled but cerebral golfer chooses to aim toward the trouble, relying on his naturally faulty swing plane to curve the golf ball back toward safety. But at that very moment the Rules of Golf are tossed aside in favor of Murphy's Law. (Whatever can go wrong, will go wrong.)

The ball starts left and then darts further left, with a physics-defying horrific hook executed in midair. Or it's a BB down the third base line, solid as a pile of bricks, zipping into oblivion in an instant. The puzzled perpetrator is left slack-jawed, wondering what became of the gentle bender, curving as pretty as a rainbow and landing gently on the short grass, that he envisioned.

It's a melancholy scenario, to be sure. The Double Crosser is trying to live with his faults. But apparently his faults can't live with him.

Solution

BY PGA PROFESSIONAL MIKE HARMON

What three things do a Double Crosser and a Cross-Dresser have in common? You can find them lurking everywhere, they're embarrassed to be caught in the act, and they'll always try and claim they've never done it before!

A double crosser is purposely trying to hit a slice or a hook and routinely hits it in the opposite direction from where he meant to. Remember that the swing path and clubface position mean everything. If you are going to play a slice or fade, make sure you are swinging to the left of your target line and that the clubface remains "open" to the target line (the imaginary line that runs from your ball to the target). A great way to practice this shot on the driving range is to imagine a tree in front of you. Better yet, try it with an actual tree in front of you. Practice a shot that would curve its way around the tree, just like shots you try when you are scrambling to get back to the fairway. Remember, it is all about the path you swing on and the clubface position at impact!

Pop-Up Boy

We love the game because we love to hit things. Hard. Make them go far. It's that simple. So the Pop-Up Peon deserves our sympathy, because far too often he steps to the tee, hoping to inflict real damage on his unsuspecting Pinnacle. But instead of launching a distance-gobbling parabola, an eye-pleasing line drive that rises into the distance, he skies it, balloons it, brings rain, hits an Elephant's Ass or a Giraffe's Backside. (Either/or—they're both high and stinky.)

As he readied himself on the launching pad, maybe the golf ball was too high. Maybe it was the golfer himself. In either case, it's a sorry scenario. From contact to touchdown, the ball might have had the same hang time as a 250-yard drive. But because it headed toward the clouds like a helium balloon instead of toward the farthest reaches of the fairway, Pop-Up Boy doesn't have to go far to retrieve it. Which is a good thing. Because he needs the energy he saves walking toward the ball to excavate it from the turf, where, more often than not, it's submerged.

MISERY METER

Solution

BY PGA MASTER PROFESSIONAL J.D. TURNER

Tee shots that are popped up are generally the result of a downswing that is too steep. The angle of impact is severe. Usually the takeaway has a similar look. The clubhead is picked up very quickly with the hands, and this abrupt angle is mirrored in the return motion. The player needs to take the club away lower to the ground with a softer, slower tempo. Using the forearms or the shoulders to initiate the swing will help. This shallowing out of the takeaway will make the return more level with the ground. A good image is the landing of an airplane. A Popper-Upper is crashing the plane into the ground. Swing with a much more subtle angle; the ball flight will be lower, and the end result will be more distance.

Shorty Driver

MISERY METER

Basketball coaches are fond of saying that you can't teach height. The same holds true with length off the tee. You either have it or you don't, and most of us don't. The causes are myriad—poor grip, poor timing, poor swing path, poor flexibility, poor coordination, poor diet, or in most cases, several of these sorry attributes in combination.

So we wheeze, lunge, grunt, and whirl. We dig in, waggle, rotate, pronate, turn our backs to the target, then swivel, and get our belt buckle facing down the fairway. All to no avail. Because while the ball often looks good as it soars off the tee, it falls from the sky like a sparrow with a stroke, thudding to rest well behind our playing companions. Wiseacres are quick to comment on these anemic efforts. "Did you hear about the new Wal-Mart they're planning?" your cart-mate asks, innocently. You reply that you haven't, and he says, "Yeah, it's being built between your drive and mine!"

That nasty nugget has been done to death in the last decade. Far better is this golden oldie, when your fellow competitor feigns concern for your feeble ball flight and offers some insidious "instruction": "You know what your problem is, don't you? You're standing too close to the ball. After you hit it!"

Solution

BY LONG DRIVE CHAMPION SEAN "THE BEAST" FISTER

You want to hit it like Fister, instead of your little sister? Well, it would help some if you were 6' 5", 235 pounds, as I am, but we're not all built like an Amana. Here are some things to work on:

Snap your wrists at impact, because they add another "power lever." Hold the club more in your fingers, as if you're picking up a pail of water. Practice making solid contact and maintaining your balance throughout the swing. Come from the inside on your golf swing for maximum power. The draw, not the fade, is the key to increasing distance, and bringing out "the Beast" within.

Tee-Box Tripper

Among the myriad ways described herein to suffer on the golf course physically, psychologically, or emotionally, the tee shot stumble is pretty innocuous stuff. But it's just slightly humiliating nonetheless.

It goes like this: a player hits an unusually good drive and gets that wonderful adrenaline rush, that release of endorphins, which accompanies a successful athletic maneuver performed under pressure. Flush with the moment's good vibes, she strides off the tee box with zest, all the while craning her neck down the fairway, admiring the ball she has just deposited in the furthest reaches of the short grass. With her head turned perpendicular, she stumbles over the tee marker. Occasionally she'll go ass-over-teakettle, but usually it's more of a lurching stagger, an ungainly ballet move that makes her companions bite their lips to stifle laughter, then quickly recover to say, "Oh Betsy, are you O.K.?"

She'll nod in assent, rubbing her barking shin, or stubbed toe, the physical discomfort a small price to pay for the wonderfully executed drive.

Of course, sometimes the same near-pratfall occurs after a terrible drive, when the player stalks off the tee box after a miserable effort, a total system failure of a drive. And because she's half-blind with annoyance,

if not anger, at her inability to make solid contact, she adds injury to insult by stumbling over the marker as a comical curtain call. And that's what you call putting a cherry on top of a garbage sundae.

Solution

BY PGA TOUR PLAYER BILLY ANDRADE

Too many hackers tee the ball in the middle of the tee box, which is a mistake. If you fade, then go to the far right side of the tee, to open up the fairway. If you hook, then go to the left side. Not only will you give yourself more room to work the ball, but you'll have a better idea of where those pesky tee markers are. And if worst comes to worst, you might want to wear shin guards.

When It's Breezy, Swing Cheesy

When a golf course is as calmly placid as a still-life painting, most hackers have all they can handle getting around without hurting themselves. But when the breeze kicks in? When the gale starts rising? That's when the shot really hits the fan.

It seems we're usually playing upwind, and the ball rises like a bottle rocket, stalls in midair, and practically blows back to our feet. A crosswind is no bargain either. The ball either gets knocked out of the sky (right-to-left wind) or sails to Madagascar (left-to-right-wind.) And putting? Never mind the distraction of the orb trembling on the green, threatening to roll a revolution the moment we pull back the putter head. The real problem is summoning the proper concentration and maintaining the necessary balance to hit a decent putt with our pant legs flapping against our shins.

But it's all worthwhile when we get to the downwind hole, isn't it? With the breeze buffeting us from behind, we're certain that a solid strike will get that ball caught up in those helping air currents, soaring like a kite down the fairway, bounding toward that mythical 300-yard mark. So we tee it high and let it fly, swinging out of our spikes to take full advantage. And when Big Bertha's bottom plate barely ticks the

top of the Titleist, and the ball wobbles, then trickles forward the length of a flagstick—only then do we embrace our Rhett Butler fates. Our chances of success in this confounding game *Gone with the Wind.*

Solution

BY PGA PROFESSIONAL BOB WOLCOTT

In the Mississippi Delta, the wind comes early and stays late. Here are three tips for both upwind and downwind playing conditions. Remember that decreasing spin will allow shots to fly further into the wind, and increasing spin will help stop shots more accurately going downwind.

To decrease the spin on the ball:
1. Choke up a couple of inches and swing normally. This will make the ball fly lower, and is a great trajectory control if you're between clubs.
2. Swing the club at three-quarters pace, which will result in less spin.
3. Aim left, put the ball further back in you stance, and put your hands ahead. Swing at about 80 percent, which will make the ball go lower without a loss of distance. Since the ball is back in the stance the club will be moving inside-out on the downswing, which is why you aim left. This is also known as the punch shot or stinger.

To increase spin on the ball:

1. Play from a normal stance but keep your hands in a neutral position, which will encourage more release of the clubhead.
2. Play the ball farther up in your stance with a full swing, which will help flight the ball higher.
3. Try to use more wrist action on your follow-through to get the ball to stop downwind.

Remember, par is good and the game is tough, so when it's breezy swing easy, and don't be cheesy!

Woodrow Wilson

The scenario: Woody Woodpecker has hooked up with three strangers and has arrived at the first par 3 on the golf course—160 yards over a pond. His three companions hit shots of varying degrees of success or failure with an assortment of middle irons. Now it's John Wooden's turn. He chooses his trusty 9-wood (downwind, he would have grabbed the 11-wood), and while he makes a couple of creaky practice swings, the trio of buddies he's joined is off to the side, elbowing each other, gawking, and smirking.

Now on the off chance this Woody Hayes hits a nice parabola with that ungainly hunk of metal, and the ball comes to rest within a shadow's distance of the flagstick, his companions will nod grudging approval at his bizarre skill, thinking of him as some sort of idiot golfing savant. But the dilemma occurs if poor James Woods misfires and pops it into the drink, or sculls it into oblivion. Then he has to chuckle nervously and lamely explain to the strangers in his midst that "normally I hit that club pretty well. I just came off it, or something."

Now if Woody Allen had dribbled one into the drink with a mid-iron of some sort, the type of club everyone else was using, his newfound companions wouldn't bat an eye—just poor contact, they'd think,

it happens to everybody. So the pressure on Woody Guthrie is unrelenting. Because not only is he desperate to hit a good shot regardless, but because of his unnatural fixation with fairway woods, because of his fear and paranoia of standard irons, he brings close and unwanted attention to himself. It's one thing to be bad. But it's a whole other thing to be bad and weird concurrently.

Solution

By PGA Professional Mike Zaranek

Too many hackers think they need to swing those long and middle irons extra fast to get them to the target. The fact is you should have the same tempo for a 200-yard 3-iron shot that you have for a 150-yard 7-iron. Just because the distance is greater, there's no need to swing harder. Let the loft of the club do the work.

Normally, tee the ball very low with an iron, maybe an eighth of an inch, so it's just hovering above the turf. You can tee it up higher if you want to impart more spin on the shot. Be sure to play the longer iron just forward of center in your stance.

That said, we're seeing more and more Woodrow Wilsons out there, and fewer Iron Byrons. Hybrid clubs and high-lofted fairway woods are easier to hit than 2-, 3-, and 4-irons. They are extremely versatile, and useful off the tee on par 3s, out of the rough, in fairway bunkers, etc. We're seeing these hybrids more and more in the bags of the elite players on the PGA Tour, so you can rest assured they're very effective.

Worm Burner

Call him the daisy cutter, the dew sweeper, or the channel digger; it doesn't matter. The names may change, but the result is always the same—a ground-hugging tee shot that screeches to a halt merely steps from where it was launched.

Well, "launched" might not be the most accurate terminology. Wormy's most fervent hope is to smack the pill toward the horizon, hurtling into an azure blue sky. But the reality is a three-hopper toward the second baseman, a bouncing, jouncing, bobber of a ball that air-brakes to a standstill in the thick grassy median that usually separates the ladies' tee from the fairway proper.

His spirits are dampened and his Foot-Joys damp as he trudges toward the muck-covered missile, soiled as a coal miner's socks. He fully expected a tee shot rising like a rocket, but instead delivered one as down-to-earth as a rosin bag. He figured he'd be taking a lengthy, windblown cart ride to the far reaches of the fairway. Instead he's walking suddenly through the sodden lea.

Solution

By PGA Professional Neel Derouen

I've been teaching golf for more than two decades, and I have given very few lessons that didn't include at least a few topped shots. To calm nervous students, I tell them a story from my past.

Back in the mid-'80s, I was looking for an instructional mentor. Several golf magazines mentioned an up-and-coming instructor in Houston, so I called him and scheduled an appointment. We worked on my game, and then I watched him teach the rest of the day. Even then he had several PGA Tour players as students, including Mark O'Meara and Brandel Chamblee, among others. Nowadays, he's best known as Tiger Woods' instructor, but this was 20 years before they became a team.

Anyway, one day Hank Haney said to me, "How about hitting some three-woods?" I must have topped 20 before getting a single one in the air. There I was, with all these PGA Tour players around, topping shot after shot. The "Worm Burner" always makes me laugh, because I had a chronic case at a very embarrassing moment in my life.

Here's how to combat the topped shot: remember that golf is a game of opposites. You must hit down on the ball to make it go up. When you try and help the ball in the air, you have a tendency to lose your spine angle and posture while standing up during the swing. The head goes up and away, the club comes up, and only the sole of the club meets the top of the ball. Stay down and go through the ball to avoid the dreaded Worm Burner.

Hacker Hall of Fame Moment

**T.C. (FOREVER KNOWN AS "TWO CHIP") CHEN
AT THE '85 U.S. OPEN
BLOOMFIELD HILLS, MICHIGAN—JUNE 16, 1985**

It was his third year on Tour, but T.C. Chen was a U.S. Open rookie in 1985. And in the first round, he had one hell of a case of beginner's luck. On the second hole, the 27-year-old Taiwan native knocked a 240-yard 3-wood into the jar for the rarest shot in the game—a double eagle. In the Open, it's no easy task making a deuce on a 127-yard par 3. But on a 527-yard par 5? This stroke of genius propelled him into the lead, the highlight of a sterling 65.

At 5'10", 140 pounds, a cynic might've thought Chen was literally and figuratively in over his head, but he backed up that opening beauty with a pair of 69s and held onto his improbable lead. He began the last day two ahead of '78 Open winner Andy North, and it was the former champ who blinked first. Chen's lead doubled to four shots through the first four holes. Then it was time to pay the piper.

On the fifth hole, he blew his approach shot 50 yards right of the green, and then left a too-delicate sand wedge in wet, clumpy grass 20 yards short of the target. Hoping to hole out for par, or get up-and-down for bogey, he chopped down on the ball. It popped straight up, as his wedge was delayed a split second by the thick grass. When the club emerged from the thatch, it hit the still-suspended ball again. The wedge flipped the ball high and to the left, where it landed 20 feet away from him onto the fringe of the green. Chen stood frozen, his face pale. He had never even seen a double-hit before, let alone made one of his own.

Including the penalty shot he incurred because of his "double trouble," he wick-whacked his way to a double par of eight, losing his entire lead in the process. His Hacker's Hangover lasted three more holes, bogeys all. In the course of just four holes, he had gone from four ahead to three behind. The final tally was "hockey sticks," also known as 77, and a second-place tie, a tortuous one shot behind the aforementioned North, arguably the least distinguished two-time U.S. Open champ in history.

As one might imagine, Chen never again came as close to Major glory. At the following year's Open, he tied for 59th. Then he missed the cut the next two years, and never played again.

It's indisputable that Chen hit two of the most memorable shots in Open history, what with the double eagle and then the infamous double-doink a couple of days later. But the fact is that his stroke of genius and then his stroke(s) of disaster added up to just 1 over par, certainly not a total catastrophe, all things considered, in a crucible like the U.S. Open. But the mind-bending experience of the shot that made him infamous was so complete, he simply couldn't function effectively the rest of the round. T.C. doesn't actually stand for Two-Chip; it's short for Tze-Chung. But it might as well have meant "Tournament Complete." Because once he pulled that "two-for-the-price-of-one" fiasco, he didn't stand a chance.

Disrobing for Dollars

MISERY
METER

Depending on how much is at stake in the Nassau, it can be a small step from Purist to Nudist. He Who Disrobes has much in common with Mr. Mud (p. 142) because he's intent on playing the ball where it lays. He also has some Aquaman attributes (p. 120), for he ends up in the drink. But this is a unique situation that only becomes a humiliation in extreme instances.

We've all seen golfers, whether in our own foursomes or playing for a million bucks on TV, take off a shoe, maybe two, to play a ball that's just inches from the water hazard. Perhaps the best-known example is poor Jean Van de Velde (p. 117), who rolled his tailored trousers to the knee while wading into Carnoustie's Barry Burn to inspect his final-hole lie at the '99 British Open, before deciding against the shot.

One of my best golf buddies, a guy with cobwebs in his wallet, was once loath to take a penalty drop when his ball was teetering on the edge of a lagoon on the left side of the fairway. He discarded his footwear, glanced around surreptitiously, and then removed his shirt, to avoid the splatter. Inspecting the silty, muck-strewn fishpond more closely, he shrugged, then took off his light-colored Bermuda shorts before wading into the thigh-high hazard. All he had on were his BVDs

(Brazen, Very Demonstrative) and a golf glove when he took a furious whack at the ball. He advanced it to safety, showering himself with detritus as we showered him with brickbats and bravos concurrently. He may have saved a stroke, he may have saved a buck, but it's harder to save face.

Solution

BY PGA PROFESSIONAL BO BOWDEN

If you play the game long enough, eventually you'll find your golf ball barely within the confines of a water hazard. The ball may be slightly submerged but playable. Play it like a buried bunker shot, but with one modification: keep the clubface square, not open, allowing the club to slice through the water under the ball, and out of the hazard. Most golfers won't take the chance on this shot for fear of getting muddy and wet. A simple solution is to tuck a towel in the right waist or hip (for a right-handed player) covering the pants and right leg. The swing will simply splash the towel, with no harm done. Or, if you're an exhibitionist, prone to stripping like a Chippendale dancer, you can just shed your golf clothes entirely.

Dyslexia

It's always been fashionable to call this confounding sport a mental test, a psychological game, a battle of nerves, or an emotional challenge. But at its essence, golf is a physical act above all, and the majority of this text showcases the collective failure of hackers to perform these acts of physicality with any degree of skill and precision.

But there are exceptions, and sometimes we fail mentally as well. Years ago I was in a tense, down-to-the-wire Nassau, with a partner who was generally quite steady. On one of the closing holes, we were both shocked when his fairway wood approach reached its apex as it went over the flagstick, airmailed the green, and landed in the woods some 30 yards behind the putting surface. I stared at him in astonishment as he looked at his club in puzzlement. "What the hell was that?" I barked, with standard sensitivity. "It was my 5-wood," he replied defensively. "I was 196 yards." I had watched the shot from the adjacent 150-yard marker, perhaps 20 yards ahead of him, and stalked back to the fairway to find the sprinkler head he had relied on. "It's 169, not 196, you idiot!"

Some years later, I came to the home hole at even par, and after a fine drive had 160 yards over a lagoon to the final green. After making solid contact

with my approach shot, I was shocked to see the ball plunge dead into the water, some 30 yards short of the intended target. I looked down in puzzlement, and was further perplexed to see the sprinkler head marked 160, as I had thought. Then I checked the club. I seethed to myself, "You grabbed a 9-iron, not a 6-iron. You idiot!"

Solution

BY DR. ELIZABETH "DOLL" MILLER

Dyslexia is a condition that involves reversing words and letters. The pathology is not in the actual oculomotor system itself and has little to do with the accurate recognition of the visual forms of words. While the occipital lobes of these patients are perfectly normal, their brains seem to be "wired" differently, making it difficult for them to break the letters of written words into the distinct sounds of our language. Bottom line: pay close attention to the yardage markers and clubheads. Don't be an idiot!

Explosion Corrosion

MISERY
METER

While the greenside bunker blast is considered by some so-called experts to be "the easiest shot in the game" (yeah, right. See "Bunker Chunker," p. 97), and a long-range fairway bunker shot, where the object is to pick the ball cleanly and send it hurtling toward a distant green, is also a skill that can be learned with some facility, nobody, I repeat, nobody, not even the sweet-swinging Sansabelt crowd collecting oversized cardboard checks most every Sunday afternoon, relishes the 50-yard sand blast.

Put an otherwise competent golfer into a sandy cavern half a football field from the flagstick, and watch him turn to strawberry jam. And what a jam it is. Too close to pick it, too far to stick it, this is golf's most hellish no-man's land. Only one in a hundred hacks can execute this most exacting shot with competence. The rest will flail away or sail away, the ball either remaining within the maw or departing for zip codes unknown, far beyond the intended target. They're left muttering in the bunker, thinking blackly that walking barefoot over hot coals or broken glass that same 50 yards of dastardly distance would be an easier assignment, and just slightly less painful.

Solution

BY WORLD GOLF HALL OF FAMER GREG NORMAN

When faced with a 50-yard sand shot, most golfers resort to a sort of power blast, taking a huge swing while also trying to minimize the distance they hit behind the ball. For obvious reasons it's a risky shot, and to pull it off, you need talent, guts, and a bit of luck.

Given the difficulty level of this particular shot, I've developed a sort of secret weapon—the slicing 8-iron. You can't hit this shot when you have a high lip to clear, but in all other situations I think it's better than the big explosion. The idea is to make a big shallow cut across the ball and slice it to the green where it will spin to the right.

You begin by setting up in an extremely open stance, while also allowing for the slice by aiming further left than with any other shot in the game. The 8-iron also needs to be wide-open and laid back, with the ball positioned off your left instep.

Figure on opening the leading edge of the clubface about 45 degrees from square. Grip the club at its full length and make a full swing. Just be sure that you strike the sand at least a couple inches behind the ball. Don't worry about digging in for too much sand, as your ball position and the open clubface will prevent that.

If you hit this shot properly, the ball will take off well left of the target and fade slightly before it hits the green. Then watch what happens. It will take one bounce, after which the sandpaper sidespin you've applied will take effect, and the ball will scoot to the right faster than any other shot.

The first time you pull this off, you'll amaze yourself. After that, you'll amaze everyone else.

Off-the-Planet Janet

**MISERY
METER**

Hard-boiled hackers learn to live with their faults. If chipping gives them fits, they'll putt from 50 yards off the green. Inveterate slicers (see p. 10) or hookers will always aim perpendicular to the fairway, hoping to veer the ball into play. But Janet's muddled mindset is best defined by the title of the popular teen movie from the mid-'90s: *Clueless.*

She doesn't know from swing to swing if the ball is going straight up toward the heavens, or will endanger every worm, snake, and mole cricket in her path. The houses on both sides of the fairway are in danger, because she can be righter than Rumsfeld, or further left than Al Franken, depending on which swing goblin shows up at that particular moment. Sometimes she dribbles a ten-footer just halfway to the hole, other times she'll drill a putt off the green and into a water hazard. Pity poor Janet, the dictionary definition of a Golf Mess in a Dress.

Solution

BY PGA PROFESSIONAL HEIDI WRIGHT

So your shots are leaving the clubface and then leaving the planet, like sorry Janet's? Try checking your distance from the ball during the setup. Golfers who tend to spray their shots often stand too far from the ball. You also may want to check your alignment and work on a consistent pre-shot routine. A helpful drill to practice is hitting balls with your feet together. This will help you swing at a speed at which you can maintain your balance, and keeping your balance is the first step in keeping the ball on the course.

The Pastor of Disaster

He's a mild-mannered sort who can plod along in a
mostly competent style. Humming a lively tune as he's
making pars, quietly reproaching himself after bogeys,
some stern self-admonishment after the occasional
double, whistling after holing an all-too-rare birdie
putt.

He'll go along swimmingly for 16, sometimes
17 holes. Now and again in moments of sustained
proficiency, it might be two full rounds. But just
beneath the surface, a debacle is waiting. Perhaps he'll
pump three tee shots consecutively into someone's
backyard. Maybe he'll get caught in some thigh-high
wispy rough just off the fairway, start hacking away
like Jack at the Beanstalk—and before he can catch
his breath, he's attempted half a dozen blows. There's
always the possibility of a flat-stick fiasco, where he
only gets the 30-footer halfway to the hole, blows
his second effort ten feet past, then tries to jam the
next one, pushing it four feet beyond, then misses the
shorty.

There are myriad ways to massacre the round, and
our poor pastor has seen 'em all. It's a shame, really.
Most every tally on the scorecard truly resembles a
golf score: 3s, 4s, and 5s, all benign. And one set of
"Boxcars."

Solution

BY SHORT GAME GURU DAVE PELZ

Even the best golfers get into rough predicaments due to errant shots or bad breaks. How they recover from those situations determines how well they will score. Our recent research indicates that golfers play two to five strokes better than their handicaps for most of each round they play. But they also have disaster holes mixed in, bringing their total scores back up to their handicap level.

Most players aren't aware that when their lie gets worse, their swings get much worse, and their shot patterns get exponentially worse. They don't know that the setup postures and swings required from trouble lies are different from those normally used and practiced, and they don't realize where their shots are going to go when they execute really bad swings from trouble lies.

Our data show golfers don't escape well from trouble lies on side hills, sloping terrain, or deep grass, or from under low-hanging tree limbs, because they try to do so using normal golf swings. Normal swings don't work from trouble lies. Golfers habitually, and unwittingly, use the exact recipe for disaster scoring: swing from an unusual posture on bad terrain, attempt a swing they've never practiced before, aim at a target they have almost no chance of reaching, and hit shots out of the frying pan into the fire and disaster!

The short answer: get the ball back on the fairway. When you're in trouble, play back to safety, laterally if necessary. Prepare to settle for bogey, maybe steal a par, but realize a double might be in the equation. Keep the calamity number, the "touchdown-and-two-point-conversion," off the scorecard.

Sideways

No, this is not a reference to the Oscar-nominated comedy film, the 2004 wine-soaked "buddy movie" starring a bunch of character actors whose names you can't recall. Propriety inhibits usage of the actual term for this most debilitating golf affliction. It's not to be said in polite company, and those who bandy the term about with impunity are cretins of the lowest order— no better than those who scream "Boo!" during your backswing, or surreptitiously toss balls out of bunkers.

There are euphemisms aplenty for this misfire, as unexpected as a heart attack, and just as welcome. Call it a hosel rocket, or in Spanish, "el ho-sel." Refer to it as a screaming lateral or a scooter. If political correctness isn't an issue, label it a Chinese hook. But a (rhymes with "crank," starts with S-H as in "Shoot! I can't believe what I just did!") is, with the possible exception of the old swing and miss, the single most devastating on-course maneuver.

Actually, it's worse than the whiff. Because when you miss outright, the only thing that's changed is your score. The ball remains in the same position. But when you hit the old "Sherman Tank" (the rhyming, Cockney version), not only has the score continued to mount, but this horrifying glancing blow, when the ball was meant to be propelled toward 12:00, but instead

has scuttled off toward 3:00, might now be deep in the underbrush, submerged in a water hazard or, ricocheting who knows where off the shinbone of your unsuspecting partner.

But the untenable new position, the unwelcome stroke addition to the scorecard, the potential of a lawsuit, rotten as they all may be, aren't the worst of it. The nastiest realization of them all is that, like the shingles, like the repo man, this wretchedness came from out of the blue. And when might it appear again? Only the golf gods know for sure, and just like the "yips," one other thing is certain. "Once you got 'em," said a wise golf pro of yesteryear, "you got 'em."

Solution

By PGA Professional Terry Florence

A wise man (perhaps a wiseguy?) once said that a shank—pardon me, to hit the ball "sideways"—was an "almost perfect shot." What he meant by that I don't know, except that you have to hit the ball perfectly to catch it right on the hosel. It's far easier to catch it on the clubface, which is a much larger area. Anyway, if we believe this sentiment, we might as well practice Russian roulette, which is a game that has less anxiety.

If you hit the ball sideways, take a deep, cleansing breath, because the next shot will be the defining moment. Stand closer to the ball. Raise the shaft angle up at address, in other words, so it's more upright. Address the ball on the toe of the clubface and try and strike the ball with the toe of the club. Using this technique, you'll hit the ball straight, not sideways.

Uneven Steven

The ball is small, the clubs are long, the swing is fast, the trouble looms. Even on the much-mentioned level playing field, much that can go wrong, will. When your feet are on the same latitude as the golf ball, making clean and crisp contact is a dicey proposition anyway. But when the ball is resting precariously on the downslope? When it's above your feet on a smallish knoll? Uphill, downhill, or side-hill lies make a difficult proposition nearly impossible for hackers across the hemisphere.

There are simple guidelines that should assist these nerve-wracking efforts. A ball below your feet should fade, if not slice. A ball above your feet should draw, if not hook, and a thinking golfer will make the necessary adjustments to compensate. But sometimes out-of-the-ordinary circumstances serve to discombobulate even the logicians among us, and the end result is a shot that's fatter than Brando, perhaps a sorry-ass swing-and-miss (see "The Whiffer," p. 77) or a misguided missile that disappears into an adjacent fairway. It's moments like these when a golfer realizes he's not just playing his opponent, but also the course. And unlike his human adversary, who's prone to much the same floundering, and can occasionally be beaten, the course will win pretty much every time.

Solution

BY PGA PROFESSIONAL BILL TOOLEY

Here in Vermont uneven lies are an everyday occurrence. While they're tricky, the right club and the proper technique make these shots less tension-filled. When the ball is on an uphill lie it will tend to fly higher and shorter than expected, so first choose a club with less loft. A downhill lie is the opposite—it will tend to fly lower and roll out longer than expected, so choose a club with more loft. Equally important in both cases is setting up with your shoulders angled with the slope of the hill. This enables you to swing with the slope and make solid contact.

When the ball is on a side-hill lie above your feet it will tend to fly to the left, or hook. The two keys to this shot are club selection and ball position. Choose a club with less loft. For example, if it is normally a wedge shot use an 8-iron. Because you are using less loft, you must gear down and use a three-quarter swing so you don't airmail the target.

Lastly, play the ball slightly farther back in your stance. These adjustments will help guard against missing with a pull or hook.

If a ball is below your feet it will tend to be a push or a fade. The adjustments for this shot are all pre-swing. First align yourself to allow for a little bit of a fade or push; next set up with a little more flex in your knees and get yourself well balanced. These adjustments should allow you to make consistent and solid contact with the ball.

The Whiffer

First things first: it happens to everybody, at least once in awhile. Even an accomplished player, confronted with a lie just inches from an immovable object, or lodged in a bush, or nestled in gnarly rough, might just swing and miss. And beginning golfers? Let's just say there are easier athletic endeavors than hitting a ball less than two inches in diameter with a rod that's three feet long, featuring a hitting surface perhaps three inches across. (This despite the fact that most modern drivers now resemble a cantaloupe on a pool cue.)

What's more embarrassing than the "whoosh" of the miss is when neophytes look up at their companions in the immediate aftermath with a sickly grin, beseeching with their eyes, hoping we'll think it was a really hard practice swing. This pathetic charade shouldn't be indulged in by anyone over the age of 11. Like mold on a shower door, this unpleasantness needs to be eradicated immediately, lest it spread to include more aberrant and unacceptable behavior like foot wedging, lie improving, and scorecard fudging. Remember; the swing-and-miss happens; it's part of the game, and not just for the unfortunate folks among us who couldn't hit lava if they fell into a volcano.

When the inevitable happens, say, "I've got to concentrate," or, "that won't happen again," or "it's

just the learning curve." But if it happens repeatedly, cropping up at the most crucial moments, and never seems to abate, you might also want to think about saying, "tennis, anyone?"

Solution

BY PGA PROFESSIONAL KEN WEYAND

Whiffing is part of sports, period. Pete Sampras won 66 professional tennis tournaments, including 14 Grand Slam events, but once in a blue moon, he'd swing and miss attempting an overhead smash. Reggie Jackson did it more than 2,500 times, and he's in the Baseball Hall of Fame! That said, there's less of a precedent in golf, because unlike a spinning tennis ball or high-velocity fastball, a golf ball is just sitting there, waiting to take its punishment.

Slow down your swing. Good golf is about the swing path and not just hitting "at" the ball. Think of staying in the same posture throughout the swing and moving the club through the ball toward your ultimate target, which should be the fairway or flagstick. If you swing over the ball you have straightened up at some point during the swing.

However, if your ball's on a tee and you swing under it, making it dribble forward a bit, don't feel bad. Lest you think this a whiff I recommend you attend a local tee-ball event. If that ball moves after the giant rubber funnel is chopped down, your son or daughter is on the way to first base. Try and tell them it's not a hit. Technically, that is not a Whiff but an Aroma. Much more sophisticated.

Wrong-Ball Ralph

There's probably an advanced algorithm, some sort of esoteric algebraic equation, to prove the following theory. But given the fact that my math training ended with high school geometry, this correspondent is in no position to prove anything.

Anyway, the postulate is this: the odds of hitting the wrong golf ball increase in direct correlation to the age of the player in question. It rarely happens to a golfer in his or her 20s or 30s. Once in a blue moon to players in their 40s, even 50s. Once you're in your 60s, those Top-Flites and Titleists start to look alike. Golfers in their 70s hit their buddy's ball almost as often as they leave their chipping clubs on the previous green, which in certain cases might be three and even four times per round. Golfers in their 80s, God bless them, are still lucky to be out there, thumping the pill through the meadow, and will tell you with little provocation they're "happy to be on the right side of the divot." In other words, above it, and not below it.

So you forgive them when they lunge after your gleaming Nike, completely forgetting they began the hole with a purple-hued Pinnacle. You shrug when they whack your brand-new Callaway, though they teed off with an orange Maxfli just five minutes before. Though their bags are full of stolen stripers,

bargain-bin castoffs, and "X-Outs," they repeatedly mistake our premium pellets for the low-grade, cart-path-scarred, slightly misshapen ammo in their own bags. And because we so rarely play under tournament conditions, there's no penalty enforced. We simply sigh, shrug, smile, clap them on the back, and say, "No big deal, Ralphie. But your ball is 60 yards back down the fairway, about 20 paces in front of the ladies' tee box."

Solution

BY PGA PROFESSIONAL J.J. SEHLKE

Here in South Florida, we have a disproportionate share of Wrong-Ball Ralphs, just as we have far too many motorists oblivious to the fact that their left-turn signals have been blinking for the better part of five miles. There are a couple of ways to combat this syndrome, best described by the late Jack Lemmon. The avid golfer and Oscar winner once said, "If you think it's hard to meet new people, try picking up the wrong golf ball."

Try the Duffy Waldorf aesthetic. The four-time PGA Tour winner has the most distinctive ball markings on Tour. His Titleists look like a box of Lucky Charms cereal—covered with hearts, moons, stars, and clovers, not to mention swirls, curlicues and who knows what else. Mark your ball in a distinctive, unmistakable fashion, and hitting somebody else's will be far less likely.

The other potential solution? Lean on your partner. No, not to make birdies, or bail you out of the hole when you're lying six in a greenside bunker, though those assists are helpful also. Have him remind you every time you leave the tee box what ball you're playing. It should almost be like an incantation, the

same way a hypnotist says, "You're getting sleepy."
If he repeatedly tells you, "You're playing a Maxfli
Noodle, you're playing a Maxfli Noodle," there's a
decent chance you won't walk up and whack the first
Precept Lady you see. Hopefully these two suggestions
will solve the problem. Either that, or eat tons of fish.
Supposed to be brain food.

Hacker
Hall of Fame
Moment

MARK CALCAVECCHIA
"SHANKS FOR THE MEMORIES" AT THE '91 RYDER CUP
KIAWAH ISLAND, SOUTH CAROLINA—SEPTEMBER 29, 1991

There's no other way to put it. Calc choked like a
Chihuahua with a chicken bone.

It was the final day of the 1991 Ryder Cup Matches,
known as "The War by the Shore," contested at Kiawah
Island's Ocean Course in coastal South Carolina. Our
Hall of Fame Hacker had been through the rigors
before; he was competing in his third Ryder Cup, with
six prior victories on the PGA Tour, including the '89
British Open, on his résumé. His singles opponent was
the then-callow Colin Montgomerie, a rookie on the
European squad. Calc vaulted to a 4-up lead with four
holes left to play, meaning that all he needed was to
tie Monty's score on any of the remaining holes in the
match to secure a valuable point for the home team.
But on 15 he made triple bogey, his lead diminishing
to 3 up with three to play. A bogey on 16, and his
lead was whittled to 2 up with two holes left. Monty,
teeing first, flinched, and dunked his tee shot in the

water on the diabolical par-3 17th. All Calc needed at that point was to find dry land with his effort, because Monty would do well to salvage bogey. Instead, he turned from putty to outright putrid, scuttle-skanking his tee ball into the pond as well, butchering his way to another triple bogey. The last hole was a foregone conclusion. Another bogey led to another hole won by Montgomerie, the match ending in a tie. Calc went to bawl on the beach. He didn't appear in another Ryder Cup for almost a decade, and when he did, he managed only a single point. Monty went onto become "the Man of the Match," playing on seven more Ryder Cup teams in succession, and never losing a one-on-one contest. In fact, through 2006 his record in Ryder Cup singles was the finest in the event's history. How different it might've turned out for the both of them if Calc had actually managed to hit the ball with the clubface on the decisive 17th.

Short Game Shenanigans

The Bunker Blader

The reason he's a poor golfer probably stems from the fact that at one time he was a poor eater. Back at grandma's house, when the extended family had gathered together and steaming platters of holiday food were all out on the table, this diffident dude resisted her heartfelt entreaty to "dig in." Same thing in the bunker.

In fact, just as he picked at his food, he attempts to pick the ball out of the sand. The end result is a startling, stupefying Scud missile of a shot, one that exits the bunker at warp speed only to end up in another sand cavern across the way, or perhaps a nearby water hazard, or the vegetation surrounding the green, or someone's backyard, or any number of undesirable places, far from his intended target: the putting surface.

But terrified of the reverse scenario (see "Bunker Chunker," p. 97), he can't help channeling the life philosophies of Twiggy, Audrey Hepburn, Kate Moss, Paris Hilton, and any other waif-like figure of the past or present—thin is in. So instead of using the leading edge, the flange, the bounce, and the sole of his sand wedge, and effortlessly cutting through the granules like a hot cleaver through Crisco, he flails away, wails

90

away, and suffers the consequences. He blades so often, he might as well be using a jackknife. Which only makes sense, because this wretched hacker is nothing but a jackass himself.

Solution

BY PGA PROFESSIONAL JOHN FERREBEE

It's right there in the dictionary between "explorer" and "exponential." But the bunker blader, whose vocabulary is as limited as his golf skills, doesn't really understand what the word "explosion" means.

In golf, the sand explosion is the excavation of the sand and ball to produce an escape from a bunker. Without the explosion, getting out of a bunker is like trying to get out of a traffic jam on the New Jersey Turnpike. It can be done, but there's luck involved, and it probably won't be pretty.

The sand wedge is designed with bounce, which will allow the club to move through the sand and explode the ball on the green. Let it work the way it should and you will see results immediately.

The Bunker Bumper

MISERY METER

There's a time and a place for this bargain-basement Band-Aid, believe it or not. Using the putter to roll or bump the ball out of a greenside hazard is the cerebral play when a golfer is confronted with a downhill lie, the sand is quite firm, and the bunker lip is minimal. But these exact circumstances are eagle-rare, which makes a typical bunker blast the shot of choice more than 95 percent of the time.

The bunker bumper shares common ground with at least a trio of other hacker types prone to humiliation. In all likelihood, she's a reformed Bunker Chunker and/or Bunker Blader, and has finally resorted to bumping because it's the least debilitating of all her evils. Like Anna Banana, she's defeated from the outset and relies on this last-gasp, woeful technique because she's run out of other options.

The sad reality is that most bunker sand is not that firm, and the Mick Jagger experience (i.e., prominent lips) is the rule and not the exception. Despite having the deck stacked against her, she'll thrash away and lash away in the sand, taking wild, ungainly whacks with her putter, trying to roll the golf ball up the slippery, granular slope, over the edge, and somewhere onto the putting surface proper. It's a harebrained and ham-handed technique, lacking subtlety, skill, and precision. But it's the only technique she's got.

Solution

BY PGA PROFESSIONAL FAITH EGLI

Putting from a bunker is like New Coke, the Ford Pinto, or going to any Pauly Shore movie … not a great idea. If you must indulge, hard-packed sand and a green that begins very close to the bunker's edge are essential. Play the ball back in your stance, press the hands forward, keep your head very still, and use extra force to propel the ball forward, rolling smoothly out of the sand and toward your target.

For a bit of loft, you can try an 8- or 9-iron, using a chipping stroke to get the ball airborne. Maybe the purchase of a putter with maximum loft in a blade style would help. Even better would be a specialty chipper, which sets up like a putter but has more loft. But the best advice of all? Limit your golf to courses that have flat, saucer-shaped bunkers, no deeper than a kiddie's wading pool.

The Bunker Chunker

Read any golf magazine. Listen to any washed-up ex-Tour pro turned television talking head. "It's the easiest shot in golf," they tell us. Nonsense.

Admittedly, some hacks have the knack. Though they can't make solid contact anywhere else on the course, they have managed to glean the ass-backwards mentality that precedes a successful bunker shot. To wit, you propel the ball out of the sand by not hitting it. Maybe it's only this sand-challenged correspondent, but doesn't it seem counter-intuitive to purposely miss the projectile in the hopes of driving it up and out of trouble? Did Babe Ruth swing behind the baseball 714 times in his storied career, or did he plonk it on the button, sending it screaming out of the ballpark? Pele didn't score 1,280 goals during his brilliant Brazilian soccer career by whiffing the ball purposely, now did he?

So for those logician golfers among us, descending into the sandy maw is a frightening quandary. We try to practice striking the ball as squarely as possible, booming it off the tee, dealing it a crisp descending blow with an iron or a solid roll with the putter. But in the bunker we're asked to do the opposite: literally swing and miss! No wonder it's a cavern of doom for so

many. Truly a Sisyphean feat, where we swing, swing, and swing again, granules flying on the green, in our shoes, in our face. The one thing that isn't flying? The damn golf ball, which remains, despite our most intense efforts, sitting placidly in the sand.

Solution

BY PGA PROFESSIONAL BARRY FLEMING

There's no need to act like a mole cricket, spending all day in the sand. For no good reason, far too many hackers descend into the bunker with their hearts thumping in fear. But the only thumping that needs to be done is that of the sand wedge into the sand, which will blow both the ball and the sand up and out of the bunker.

Here's what to do: set up with the ball positioned on the instep of your front foot, so the club will scoot underneath and past it. Open the clubface slightly so it won't dig in too deeply, set up just left of the target, and make a normal wedge swing. It's helpful to visualize the ball on a tee, which is buried in the sand. When you swing, try and clip the tee, right beneath the head. This will help you achieve the proper depth into the sand.

Here's a food analogy that might be of help: picture your ball as the yolk of a fried egg sitting on the sand. Hit some shots, working on removing the entire egg, not just the yolk, from the sand. With a little practice, you can go from out of the sand, onto the green, and maybe even into the hole. And turning from a Bunker Chunker to a Bunker Dunker is one of the best feelings in golf.

The Dink

In how many ways should we stand in awe of Tour pros? We can admire their titanic drives, deft touch in bunkers, and laser-guided iron play, among other attributes. Here's another. How many times have you seen Tiger Woods or any other television mainstay battling in the heat of a tournament, standing over a decisive putt, staring at the hole, contemplating the line, factoring the speed? Meanwhile he's insouciantly waving his putter back and forth, millimeters from the ball, as though trying to shoo away a pesky fly. How on earth do they "do the wave" with such nonchalance?

They're trying to keep their arms loose just prior to attempting their putt, but it looks as though they have a screw loose, so close to the ball do they oscillate their putters. And almost never, with only the rarest of exceptions (see Introduction) does the club contact the ball inadvertently. Now compare the Tour guy to the poor guy, hapless hacker, sad slacker, who, while actually staring down at his ball, not gazing at the cup or the intended line, manages to dink his ball by accident during his tentative, palsied, practice motion. And in this case, with apologies to philosopher René Descartes ("I think, therefore I am") the verb becomes a noun. "I dink, and therefore am a dink."

Solution

By PGA Professional Chris Carter

Anyone who has inadvertently made contact with the ball on a practice stroke knows just how embarrassing this can be. Luckily our buddies usually give us a pass and let us replace the ball without penalty, though they think we're a dink for doing it. But if you're in a tournament? Playing some hard cases? In the middle of a high-dollar Nassau? Don't expect any charity then.

Players take practice strokes to get the feel of how much effort is going to be required to hit the putt. Try standing on the extended target line with the ball between you and the hole, looking at the cup while taking a few strokes. For example, if it's a 20-foot putt, stand 5 feet behind the ball, so you're 25 feet from the target. This allows your "mind's eye" to feel the effort required to make the putt. Your eyes will be level, and your chances of accidentally dinking the ball will be reduced to zero. Davis Love III (who had to learn the hard way) and many other Tour players have gone to this method.

The Double Hitter

We don't know why it happens—or, more importantly, why it has to happen to us. It's as unforeseen as an earthquake and, within the context of a golf round, almost as calamitous. We might be in a bunker, maybe some thick greenside rough, occasionally on the tight weave of the fairway, not far from the putting surface. It's almost always a finesse shot that we're attempting, and, if they're uttered quickly, there's little difference between the words "delicate" and "double hit."

When it happens, we go slack-jawed at our own ineptitude, blindsided by our bungling nature. But you know who's truly amazed? The Whiffer lurking in the foursome. She can't even hit it once, but just watched you hit it twice in an instant, two distinct "clicks" in a nanosecond, a real "two-for-one-swing" special.

For baseball lovers, there's nothing quite like a long, lazy day at the ballpark, looking back to the halcyon days of yesteryear, and the prospect of attending a doubleheader. And for golf lovers, there's nothing quite as jarring, disconcerting, or ruinous, to both the mindset and scorecard, as the prospect of becoming a double hitter.

Solution

BY PGA PROFESSIONAL DAVE CHRISTENSON

Thankfully this shot is as rare as Steak Tartare, but it can make you equally sick to your stomach. A double hit most often occurs when the ball is resting in a wicked lie, and a player takes extra care in trying to finesse the perfect shot.

Avoiding double trouble begins with the setup. It is important for right-handed golfers to keep the weight on the left leg (the opposite goes for lefties.) With your weight in the proper position, now simply grip down an inch or two on the handle of the club. This helps shorten the backswing, allowing the transition into the ball with proper acceleration. Maintaining speed and acceleration in the downswing will allow the club to contact the ball as expected, eliminating the dastardly double hit. This will keep both blood pressure and handicap index at manageable levels.

In Love with Loft

His golf goals are lofty, but unfortunately so are his scores. And the primary reason is the lofty clubs he bull-headedly chooses around the greens. Quick-study golfers learn that bouncing and rolling the ball toward the target is normally the most effective play. For every Phil Mickelson, capable of rocketing a flop shot toward the heavens and having it stop like Velcro-covered duct tape next to the pin, there are ten thousand Ill Sickelsons who, attempting the same maneuver, will scull the ball 150 yards, or barely move it a foot.

So if there's no wetland, water, or waste area to navigate, most semi-competent plodders learn to bump that hybrid, bat that 8-iron, bang the putter from the fringe toward the flagstick, all in the attempt to minimize outright calamity. But the Loft Lover keeps swinging that gap wedge, grabbing his attack wedge, attempting to feather his 64-degree wedge in there tight. But the results are rarely pretty. Not only does he have too much loft, he also has L.O.F.T. (Lack of Freaking Talent).

Solution

BY PGA PROFESSIONAL MIKE MITCHELL

Hackers often pull out a wedge with 60 degrees for a shot that requires a 6-iron. The real rule is getting it on the ground as quickly as possible and letting it roll. Minimum air time—maximum ground time.

I'll kneel down with students as we gently toss balls underhand to a target. The student never attempts to lob one over Fenway Park's Green Monster, yet they often try to on the course. A lower shot generally requires less motion and backswing, which increases the chance for solid contact. The big swings with an open clubface should be left to "Lefty."

Play the ball back in your stance; get both the shaft and your weight forward; then deliver a crisp downward blow with a shorter, simpler motion. Get used to hitting 5-, 6-, 7-, 8-, or 9-irons, or a pitching wedge, for shots inside of 20 or 30 yards. The more shots in your arsenal, the stronger a player you become.

On in Two, Off in Three

There might be more humiliating things that occur on the golf course, most involving some sort of bodily injury, but there are few more disheartening things than this sorry scenario. Here's the scene: an excited hacker manages to hit a par-4 green in regulation, an occurrence as common as the removal of a page from the calendar.

Now this rare approach shot wasn't exactly a laser at the flagstick, but instead has come to rest a good distance from the hole, which is situated somewhere near the edge of the green. Quivering with excitement at the prospect of an honest-to-goodness birdie putt, the overeager golfer jabs at the ball like he's trying to drive a nail into a baseboard. The result? The startled orb skitters past the hole at warp speed, careens off the edge of the green itself, and trundles down into a collection area 10 or even 20 yards away. Elation gives way to abomination; the putter is mournfully set aside while a chipping club is fetched from the bag; and the hard-luck hack is left muttering, "on in two, off in three."

Solution

By PGA Tour Player Brad Faxon

I've seen a million hackers spend hours on the range before a Pro-Am, and then roll two quick putts before heading to the tee. No wonder they have "hammer hands." Before playing, roll some long putts in both directions—up and down the hill, with left-to-right and right-to-left break. Remember that wind, slope, grain, and grass texture are all part of the putting equation. Proper grip pressure is essential. Hold the putter tight enough so the head won't twist, but soft enough so if someone tries to pull the putter out of your hands your arms will have some "give." Lastly, there are no shortcuts. Competent putting takes time. Give it your full attention, or you'll have plenty of time to think about your "greens neglect" when you're walking down into the swale, preparing to chip the ball back up onto the green.

The Yipper

Naysayers abound, thinking there's nothing inherently athletic about golf, but they are wrong, dead wrong. Making a sound, repeatable, powerful golf swing is about talent, timing, tempo, and dexterity. Those who are too old, injured, restricted, infirm, feeble, or uncoordinated will suffer. But not so with putting, particularly close-range putting. Anyone from age 5 to 95 has the physical wherewithal to make a two-foot putt. But some horrified hackers, much to their ongoing shame and dismay, cannot.

Lacking the requisite degree in physiology or biomechanics, all that can be offered is a set of platitudes. It's nerves. It's the dread of missing the "gimme," and the shame that will ensue. It's the neurons firing in a discombobulated fashion. It's a twitch, a spasm, a sudden, uncontrollable convulsion between bringing the putter back and then bringing it forward. Who knows what it is, other than it stinks?

And when the ball remains in the daylight instead of the darkness, and the shoulders of this sorry schlep sag in dejection, it feels like a knife between the shoulder blades. And you know what makes the knife twist? When the disbelieving opponents, either out of glee or ghoulishness, start celebrating greenside. "He missed the putt! We win! Yippee!"

Solution

BY CHAMPIONS TOUR PLAYER LOREN ROBERTS

Too many hackers put undue pressure on themselves when they get in that "throw-up zone," two or three feet from the hole. At that distance, just visualize the ball going in the hole like you saw it when you were lining it up from behind. Just stroke the putt the proper distance, concentrate on the correct speed of the putt, and the ball will find the hole practically every time. It's like playing a simple game of catch from short range. You don't really worry about aiming the baseball. If you toss it the proper distance, not over your partner's head, or into the dirt, you'll hit the target every time. Listen to this advice, and you'll do fine. After all, they call me the Boss of the Moss, not the Boss of the Miss.

Hacker Hall of Fame Moment

JEAN VAN DE VELDE
HE "SACRE BLEU" HIS CHANCE AT THE '99 BRITISH OPEN
CARNOUSTIE, SCOTLAND—JULY 18, 1999

The feckless Frenchman had his spikes and socks off, his tailored trousers rolled up near the knee, hands on hips, standing in the "wee burn" fronting the final green at the 1999 British Open. The refrain from the 1980 Talking Heads song "Once in a Lifetime" might've been rolling though his mind: "How did I get here?"

Here's how: he stood on the 72nd hole at Scotland's Carnoustie (dubbed "Car-Nasty") with a three-shot lead. A double bogey six would secure the championship, and golf immortality. (As a pundit remarked later, "He should've been able to make a six wearing a mask, snorkel, and fins.") Van de Velde blew his drive well right, but the ball was improbably, fortuitously, resting safely. Instead of playing back to the fairway with a wedge, then wedging on and two-putting for what would have been a two-shot win, he inexplicably hit a 2-iron toward the green. "I wanted to finish like a champion," he said later, miserably.

His approach sailed right and unluckily banged off a grandstand railing, landing in thick fescue. He hacked from the hay, and the third shot found the water which is where this tale began two paragraphs above. His comical turn as "Shoeless Jean" ended quickly. After inspecting his submerged lie close up, for a brief delusional moment thinking he might play his fourth shot from within the stream, he reconsidered. He wisely decided to remove the ball from the water and took a penalty stroke. He ultimately bungled his way to a seven, which landed him in a play-off, which of course he stood no chance of winning. He remains a footnote to golf history, instead of an out-of-the-blue, fairy-tale Major champion.

It was a tough weekend all around for handsome, dark-haired, 30-something sportsmen. The day before the Frenchman's antics, John F. Kennedy Jr. died piloting his own plane. While Van de Velde's implosion was disastrous, at least it wasn't fatal. But the Talking Heads analogy takes us one step further, because for "shoulda-coulda-woulda" Jean his chance for the brass ring (and Claret Jug) was truly "Once in a Lifetime."

Injuries, Emotional Imbalances & Other Indignities

Aquaman

MISERY
METER

Retrieving a submerged ball from a precarious spot is a lot like heeding a volatile stock tip, or attempting to bite off a dogleg by aiming over the trees. In all three cases, the guiding principle is fear versus greed.

Most hacks are resigned to blowing through balls like Liz Taylor went through husbands—quickly, regularly, and with little emotional bond. But some oddballs get unnaturally attached, treating that discolored pellet like some sort of family heirloom.

So they teeter at water's edge, they strain, they use the extra, extra long ball retriever, they'll go so far as to suggest a human chain. And sometimes they go too far, literally. For every thousand safe extrications, only one sorry (soon to be sodden) soul will actually topple in. But it happens.

Years ago, I knew a dentist at my old club in New England. I wasn't present at the moment that could have easily won the grand prize on *America's Funniest Home Videos,* had that show been in existence at the time, but the story swirled around the grounds for months. His ball had plopped into the middle of the watery ditch bisecting the 13th (notice the symbolism?) fairway. He actually had the temerity (stupidity) to inch out on a narrow drainage pipe running perpendicularly across the water. The result—slipping

spikes, windmilling arms, yelped curses, and a headlong splash—made him a legend. He disappeared from the club soon after, but there's a chance his resignation had to do with something other than just embarrassment. Perhaps his dental practice was ailing, and he couldn't afford both club dues and the dry-cleaning bill concurrently.

Solution

BY PGA PROFESSIONAL JEFF YOST

Real Golfers Don't Use Ball Retrievers. As the saying goes, "Don't bet a guy with a 1-iron, and don't pick a partner with a ball retriever." Now, much as with hitting quality golf shots, fundamentals that focus on club selection and balance are essential to avoid an unwanted drenching.

Proper club selection is crucial. Loft is critical for being able to cradle the ball when it is nestled in the weeds surrounding a pond. However, straining with too much loft and not enough length will only cause problems. Just as some par 5s cannot be reached in two, some golf balls are destined to remain in a watery grave. Know what your clubs can do and what you can do with your clubs.

Use your toes to help control the forward lean, much in the way a kangaroo uses its tail to keep from falling over. As with the golf swing itself, practice is essential. Stroll along every hazard, and search for golf balls close to shore. Use of polarized sunglasses will help spot balls others may miss.

Lean toward your target, club in your dominant hand, with the face of the club pointed toward the sky. Slide the clubface under the target area, and slowly raise the target with the larger arm muscles, guiding the ball steadily toward the shore. Then use the classic scrape motion to remove the submerged orb. Don't attempt the "hero" maneuver very often. If you attempt to do too much and become an inadvertent "Aquaman," particularly here in Charleston, where gators roam the ponds, a golf ball might not be the only thing you lose.

The Assassin

Golf a genteel game? Think again. The ball's a dimpled weapon, rock-hard, and it comes off the clubface at more than a hundred miles an hour. With all the harebrained hackers out there, bringing new meaning to the phrase "loose cannon," it's a wonder people aren't maimed or killed more often. And this correspondent knows of what he speaks.

More than a decade back, my own misfire off the tee box almost caused catastrophic injury to one of my best pals. I was aiming at 12:00, trying to bisect the fairway of a tree-lined par 4. Happy Jack was standing safely, we both presumed, at 10:30 or 11:00, perhaps 20 yards ahead of the tee box at the ball washer. I pull-hooked a crushing liner that hit him in the upper pectoral muscle. He leapt off the ground in shock and pain, a vertical leap the world hadn't seen since Michael Jordan was a Carolina Tarheel.

After a solid five minutes of writhing histrionics, Happy Jack tried to continue playing, but couldn't get the club back anywhere near parallel. He chipped and putted for a few holes, then just putted, and eventually motored back to the clubhouse for a six-pack to go. That night we were at a party, and that bruise, with dimple imprints clearly visible on the skin, turned more colors than a Hawaiian sunset. Jack gave up the

game shortly thereafter, ostensibly because his wife gave birth to twin boys. Did his on-course near-death experience have anything to do with the decision? He still won't say, but his love of golf, like the "Titleist" imprint that briefly adorned his chest, faded away.

Solution

By PGA Tour and Champions Tour Player Fred Funk

They said it must have been embarrassing to be out-driven by Annika Sorenstam and have to wear a pink skirt on national television, both of which I endured at the 2005 Skins Game. But it's not as embarrassing as practically knocking over your best pal like a bowling pin when he's minding his own business next to the ball washer.

Keep your posture perfect to avoid the hard pull off the tee. If you stand erect and lose your spine angle on the backswing, you have to make an on-the-fly readjustment on the downswing to avoid whiffing. Make your swing without losing the spine angle. That way you won't lose your golf ball, or for that matter, your golf buddies, nearly as often.

Everest

It can be a single shot, an entire golf course, or something in between. It's a mental hurdle, a psychological block, a barrier that can't be surmounted in your round, a fractured track-line that causes a scorecard derailment. Why "Everest?" It's a hump you just can't get over.

There are nearly as many forms of this debilitation as there are stripers on the driving range. It might be just one swing of the club, like that mocking little par-3 tee shot over water. Sometimes it's 400 yards of contemptuousness; the dogleg par 4 with OB stakes down the entire right side. It's often a series of consecutive holes, a devilish "Amen Corner" of the psyche, dangerous as a minefield—or perhaps "mind-field" would be a better choice of words.

Why can we play many, even most of the holes on any given course with confidence? Or, at least, without abject terror? Nevertheless, past psychological baggage causes us to irrationally fear a shot, a hole, or a series of holes that truly might be no harder or more daunting than any situation preceding or following. Unlike the iconic mountain providing the name of this Humiliation's title, "Everest" won't actually kill you. But it will make you light-headed, cause your heart to pump wildly, and, quite often, make you freeze.

Solution

By PGA Professional Mike Dynda

The key to scaling Everest is focusing on the process itself, not the end result. It's been said many times, but it really does come down to one shot at a time. This concept will help a tournament leader sleep more soundly on the overnight lead, and a college golfer play more freely, without worrying about letting his or her teammates down.

I have witnessed this phenomenon repeatedly at the Montgomery County Amateur Championship, a high-profile event held annually at my Philadelphia club. A fine local amateur named Buck Jones, a former Philadelphia Publinks champion and U.S. Senior Amateur contestant, almost always holds the lead after round one in this annual two-day tournament.

Unfortunately, his game disintegrates early during the final round, contested at my home course, Blue Bell Country Club. He usually recovers in the homestretch but finishes second or third, a shot or two short. Blue Bell's front nine is his Everest.

Here's a personal example. Years ago I'd be in contention annually at one of our Philadelphia sectional events. On a certain back-nine hole I would invariably snipe the ball into the left woods and make double bogey. Every year I would recall my failure, and it would repeat. I had a mental block, pure and simple. What I eventually learned was that the brain doesn't differentiate between "do" and "don't." I was thinking, "Don't hit in the woods," but the brain only heard "woods."

When I learned to focus my efforts on where I wanted the ball to go, instead of obsessing about where it shouldn't, I started striping it down the fairway. So what's the process? Focus on your pre-shot routine. Visualize where you want the ball to go and concentrate on the target. The fourth is the hardest to learn, but vitally important: learn not to care so much. It's not life or death. Don't get wrapped up in the result, but instead focus on the process of hitting a quality shot. Then you'll easily scale Everest, and you won't even need oxygen.

Greta Garbo

Just like the '30s film star, his mantra is "I want to be alone." Consider this curious case, concerning one of my golf-writing chums. Beanie was whapping and slapping at this Southern resort course in reasonable fashion for 17 and a half holes. That is to say, his concluding tally was headed for a number well north of body temperature, but far below the boiling point of water (212 degrees Fahrenheit, for the science-challenged).

Anyway, as we approached the final green, Beanie started misfiring like a 1975 AMC Gremlin. He took nearly a dozen blows to find the bottom of the cup from 50 yards away. I was safely on the closing par 5 in regulation, and while Beanie was laboring to find the putting surface with shots seven through eleven, I was enjoying the classical strains emanating from the wedding ceremony about to commence, taking place on the club's elegant stone patio, some 50 yards above us. Then it hit me like a Russell Crowe–thrown telephone: Beanie was falling to pieces because he thought the formal-clad wedding attendees seated above us, anticipating the bride's arrival and facing away from the 18th green, were actually interested in his below-average golf skills. Granted, most of us

aren't real keen on an extended audience. We wonder internally how the hell Tour pros can hit quality shots into greens surrounded by packed grandstands. But there are some golfers who detest scrutiny of any kind, beyond that of their own foursome. Had Thoreau ever wielded a brassie or niblick in addition to a fountain pen, he might've added to his famous quote: "Most men lead lives of quiet desperation. And prefer to golf in isolation."

Solution

BY PGA PROFESSIONAL DOUG GOUBAULT

Never mind Thoreau. How about a famous Bill Clinton quote instead: "I feel your pain."

Nobody likes to look foolish in front of other people. It's just that the Greta Garbo types on the golf course take it to the extreme. In most sports, adrenaline can be your friend. The play is continuous, and is full not just of action, but of instantaneous reaction. But even within a convivial foursome, golf offers solitude, and too much time to think, between swings, about what could go wrong.

So a couple of encouraging thoughts for all the Greta Garbo golfers of the world: remember that every avid player, of any ability level and from any era, from Jack Nicklaus to Jack Nicholson, from Babe Zaharias to Babe Ruth, has flubbed countless shots. And, outside of a massive, Major championship meltdown like that of Jean Van de Velde nobody can remember them two days later. It's the same philosophy you need to impart to your friends who are leery of using caddies. Explain that no matter how bad at golf they think they are, the caddie has always seen somebody worse. And lastly, don't be afraid of messing up in front of others for this simple reason.

If you're observed by a non-golfer, they might not realize how bad the shot really is. And if you're being watched by a golfer, they know how darn hard the game can be.

Jack the (Pants) Ripper

MISERY
METER

You don't have to be hefty, but it sure helps. Perhaps those cream pies have gone to your thighs, your calves are more like cows, there's a moose in your caboose, a bit too much junk in the trunk. The unexpected happens when you squat to see the putting line, pull a ball out of the cup, or bend down to pick up a tee. The sound is often identical to that of a hearty burst of flatulence, and the first reaction of one's playing partners will be to back away a few steps from the detonation. In a moment they'll realize it's safe to breathe, and, depending on the comfort level and camaraderie of the group, either embarrassed silence or gales of tear-inducing laughter will ensue.

Philosophers have long discussed the sound of one hand clapping. But the sound of one pant flapping in the breeze is less abstract.

Solution

BY FORMER PGA TOUR PLAYER CHARLIE RYMER

Being a man that is 6' 4" and somewhere just south of 300 pounds I have extensive experience in the area of crotch "blowouts." I've sewn up more fabric in my day than Betsy Ross. This ailment affects us "full-figured" folk, which I define as anyone who has been laughed at while asking for appropriate-sized clothing at the local golf shop. Having studied the textile sciences at Georgia Tech, I'm familiar with the effect of methane gas on clothing fibers. The combination of methane gas, fiber degradation caused by constant grating of the thighs, and friction heat is a recipe for disaster.

Avoid bending over or squatting, to minimize stress in the trousers. Use a blade putter, so you can scoop the ball out with the toe. Hope your group is liberal, and lets you pick up those pesky two- and three-footers. If the ball falls in the hole by accident, feign a back injury, walk stiff-legged to the hole, and ask someone to retrieve the ball for you.

In my days on tour I concocted a clever plan to battle this malady. My pants were tailored with a Teflon coating in the crotch lining, but make sure the tailor understands that the Teflon faces out to minimize friction, and not toward the skin. I accidentally wore a pair with the Teflon liner backwards in a 36-hole U.S. Open qualifier. I was very fortunate to eventually recover and go on to have children.

Mr. Mud

Not everyone can play good golf. But everyone can play real golf, though the hackers among us willing to thoroughly abide by the rules of the game are as rare as double eagles. And while many golf rules are a combination of esoteric and persnickety, there's at least one basic tenet that should always apply: play the ball down. It's a dying art outside of the professional tours though, and rolling, fluffing, massaging, propping, and manicuring the ball have become de rigueur.

So "Muddy Waters" earns our respect, because he'll whack that pellet from wherever it lies, regardless of the circumstances. It might be sitting in a damp and muddy patch of earth adjacent to the cart path. It could be squelchy turf just inches from the water hazard. It might be oozing rough adjoining some ground under repair. But playing it as it lies is important to our hero, because he prides himself on playing "real golf." So he'll gingerly take his stance, give a resigned sigh, often close his eyes at the moment of impact, and flail away, hoping for a meaningful advancement of the ball. Sometimes he gets lucky, but usually he just gets mucky. And though he's now sartorially sorry, we admire his grit, literally. To this king of crud, this prince of Tide, we offer a heartfelt toast: here's mud in your eye!

Solution

BY PGA PROFESSIONAL CHRIS MARTINEZ

In the tropical desert of Cabo San Lucas, Mexico, rain is a rarity. "Mr. Mud" visits as often as Santa Claus—once a winter. During the late summer rainy season, though, he's been known to make an occasional appearance.

The lie of the ball dictates the type of shot needed, for golfers should strive to take what the golf course gives them, instead of trying to do "the impossible." For example, if the ball is set down below the level of the fairway in a sludgy old divot, then it should be played slightly back in the stance. This will insure a more descending blow, in an effort to hit the ball first. Consequently, the ball will come out with a lower trajectory than normal.

Many players expect to hit the same type of shot from all types of lies. But it's a difficult task for the average player to hit a towering draw when the ball is sitting in a low-laying, muddy lie or wet divot. Although the player might make the necessary swing shape to create a high draw, the result is that the club is coming into the ball at too shallow of an angle, creating a fat shot that advances more mud than ball.

With a level lie in soft or wet conditions, strive to sweep the shot by making sure the ball position is either in the middle, or forward-of-middle in the stance. In firm or dry conditions, strive to make a divot after contact. And lastly, remember to wear dark clothes when there's mud on the golf course. The stains don't show as easily!

Rapture on the Range, Remorse on the Course

This common Humiliation in a nutshell: Davis Love on the range, and Courtney Love on the course.

What causes this change from aptitude to ineptitude, the transformation coming in the space of a 30-second walk from practice tee to tee box? It's like looking at the "Evolution of Man" chart, but in reverse. After a dozen feathery wedges surrounding the 100-yard marker and two dozen laser-guided drivers bounding past the 250-yard sign, Jekyll stands erect and proud like any card-carrying Homo sapiens; he's a man who really knows how to use his tools. But he shrinks a little after that first wayward drive, he hunches a bit after that scuttled iron; he shrivels after that opening three-putt; and by the time he's on the second tee, he's little more than a Neanderthal in Nikes. Poor, pitiful Jekyll has 17 holes in front of him; his confidence has evaporated as his game suddenly vanished, and he's got nowhere to Hyde.

Solution

By PGA Professional Andrew Rice

Even though the actual distance might be negligble, it's often said that the longest walk in golf is from the practice ground to the first tee. If you are one of the many who go from rapture to remorse, rarely transferring your true ability to the links itself, the problem is that your practice and warm-up sessions are nothing like the way you play.

The key is to "play golf" while practicing. This can be done by visualizing each shot on the range as if it were on the course. Picture various situations you may encounter in the opening holes, seeing both target and trouble, before pulling the trigger. This exercise mentally prepares you for what you are about to encounter on the course.

Keep in mind that you should vary the clubs you hit, vary the targets you hit to, and always use your pre-shot routine during this exercise. Try this drill on the range, and you will find yourself better prepared to deal with the demons of the links!

Rick O'Shea

Anyone who knows which end of their driver to grab onto has been caught on the ass end of this sorry scenario.

Your tee shot ends up in the woods. The safe play is laterally, or an angled shot toward the fairway, which will leave a short iron to the green, and perhaps a chance to get up-and-down for par. But the heart pounds and the adrenaline courses regardless. Because with either a sniping hook between the tree trunks or a soaring fade, a Scud missile beneath the branches or a helium shot over, the green can actually be reached.

"The smart play would be out to the fairway," you chide yourself, as the do-or-die moment approaches. But though your odds of an ace on the next par 3 are only slightly longer than your chances of knocking this ball through the various hardwood obstacles in your path and onto the putting surface, all you can think of is the looks of astonished admiration you'll get from your playing companions should you pull this miracle shot off.

You'll inevitably flinch, of course, at the moment of impact, and the results will be unfortunate. The best of the worst cases: you remain stymied in the trees, and you have to think about the stratagem all over again. There's also an excellent chance you'll carom

off the hardwood, ending up out-of-bounds, adding stroke-and-distance to your misery. But the worst case of all? The vicious rebound, which might catch you in the thigh, or worse, the eye. (I know a low handicapper who knocked out his four front teeth with these attempted heroics.) And if the ball hurtles backwards, impacting below the beltline? The hapless hacker will be left gasping for breath, doubled over, saying literally and figuratively, "oh, nuts!"

Solution

BY PGA PROFESSIONAL ALAN CARTER

Up here in the Canadian wilds, there are ample opportunities to ricochet. You can bounce one off a massive Canadian fir, slam one off a slab of granite, maybe even off the flank of a coyote, elk, or grizzly bear if you've strayed from the fairway. It looks like there's a lot of room; you haven't hit a hook in weeks or maybe ever, but put a tree in front of you and bingo! The ball ends up coming right back at you faster than it left your club every time. If there was ever a way to save a few strokes it would be to use your head, take your lumps like a full-grown golfer, and simply get the ball back in play, nothing more. You could be real clever and aim right at the tree, because you never hit it where you want to anyhow. But somehow you'll end up hitting maybe the first perfect shot of your life, and you'll be diving out of the way of the rebound. Be smart, take your punishment, and chip the ball back out into the fairway where you can make a full swing without hurting yourself or anyone else.

The Root of All Evil

The game is tough enough when dealing with the
pitfalls you can easily discern—water, sand, OB stakes,
and the like. But what of the guerrilla hazards that
sneak up out of nowhere?

    This correspondent once had the phenomenally bad
luck of engaging an inch-thick tree root in a little game
of "chicken." It was a mismatch from the opening bell;
tree root in a TKO. I'm not angling for a rematch, but it
wasn't a fair fight. This wasn't your standard tree root,
lying plainly visible. Had that been the case, declaring
an unplayable lie would've been the least offensive
option, and a penalty stroke along with the drop away
from the root would've been the penance. Or at least
a thin little defensive shot might've been attempted,
holding the club lightly and attempting to play out
laterally. Neither of these options was a consideration,
because this root was as devious as they come, a real
predator. It lay there perfectly camouflaged by a
thin layer of autumn leaves, biding its time, patiently
waiting for an innocent and unlucky victim. After
the wildly inaccurate tee shot preceding this most
unwelcome episode of "Roots," it was good fortune to
have even found the ball at all, in what looked like a
decent lie, with a reasonable stance, and an unimpeded
line to the green. Out came a long iron in an attempt

to reach the putting surface, nearly 200 yards away. The club came down in a blur, met that damned root, and stopped dead. It was like kicking a brick wall in sandals.

Walking up the fairway in a daze, my right hand vibrating with pain, I was sick with the realization that some serious damage had been inflicted. In the weeks that followed, X-rays, bone scans, ice, heat, ultrasound, acupuncture, and a mild electric charge called iontophoresis became part of the daily routine. The soft tissue damage had me shaking lefty, and far more inconveniently, off the links for months afterward.

The incident is thankfully now a mostly faded memory, and while the injury ran its course, there were two residual effects. The first relates to how carefully I now inspect any lie involving underbrush or any type of potential tree trouble. The second is that Arbor Day remains at the top of my list of least favorite holidays.

Solution

By LPGA Tour Player Reilley Rankin

I know all about injuries on the golf course. And unfortunately, I know far too much about injuries that can keep you off the golf course.

Roots are dangerous, pure and simple. When I play for fun, with my family or friends, there's no question at all about taking a free drop away from a root.

My golf balls are marked R/R, which has significance far beyond my initials. Course management is something I'm constantly working on, so those letters serve as a constant reminder that golf is a game of risk versus reward. But when you're tangling with a tree, the risk of injury far outweighs the potential reward of hitting a green in regulation, or advancing the ball well down the fairway. So hit the ball laterally, or even backwards. Swing the club gingerly. Take an unplayable lie if you must. Your hands have more bones than any other part of the body, so don't go for broke, because "broke" might take on long-term and painful significance if you do.

Tee-Totaled

A non-playing friend's non-playing wife was amused when I told her I tweaked my back on the golf course. As a dispassionate observer, looking at a slow-moving game played mostly in carts, with no defense, contact, or overt exertion, she was surprised to hear one could actually get hurt playing the game. How little she knew.

Back, neck, and wrist issues are common. Blisters on fingers and feet are a recurring theme. Sunburn, sand in the eyes, stepping in a hole, being blindsided, and getting bowled over by a wayward shot (see "The Assassin," p. 125) are all possibilities. Flipping a cart, finding fire ants, or whacking a root can all lead to unexpected golf course trauma.

Here's one you don't see every day, or even every decade: years ago I was peg-less striding to the tee box. "Brad, toss me a tee, will you?" I said with insouciance, my concentration on the tree-lined fairway ahead of me. The weightless little weapon was lobbed to me end-over-end. I snatched it from the air unthinkingly, and the palm-puncturing that followed was as painful as it was unexpected. "Firecracker!" or something to that effect—I yelled in disbelief. The wound was minuscule, practically bloodless. But its mid-palm

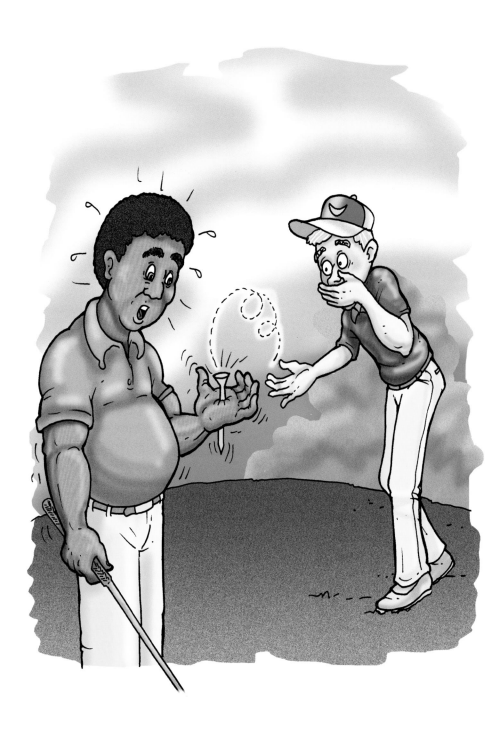

location, as central as a bull's-eye, prevented me from gripping the club, and consequently from finishing the round. Lacking the ability to play left-handed, I had nothing left to do but knock back a few cold ones and ride along for the duration. I caught a nice beer buzz that afternoon, all because I was turned into a teetotaler.

Solution

BY PGA PROFESSIONAL MIKE HAYES

You couldn't have been tee-totaled 115 or so years ago, because until the end of the 19th century, golfers used a small pile of sand to tee the ball. Of course, late in the 1800s, you had other worries: tuberculosis, smallpox, and polio, to name three, but I digress.

How to avoid an unexpected tee-box stabbing event? There are several solutions. The most obvious is to always have tees on your person, so nobody's tossing one in your direction. If your trousers have holes in the pocket (which is why the tees might've slipped out, which is why you asked your buddy to throw you one in the first place), a standard tee fits comfortably behind the ear. Speaking of standard tees, try a newfangled model. Whether a brush tee, a zero-gravity tee, or a rocket golf tee works any better than the industry standard is a matter of debate. But they could well be less dangerous flying through the air. Another thought: though we wear our golf gloves on the non-dominant hand, the thin leather layer of the glove will serve as protection from a potential puncture. It's also a lesson in dexterity, so learn to catch a thrown tee in your "other," or gloved hand, instead of barehanded.

Lastly, just as in the game itself, technique can always be improved. Don't snatch a tossed tee out of the air, like you would catch a set of car keys, for example. Face the thrower palm up, and let the tee fall into your hand, without closing your fist when it arrives. You wouldn't snatch a bowie knife, Buck, or jackknife out of the air, and we've learned that a renegade golf tee, at least once in a great while, can also be a semi-dangerous projectile.

Hacker Hall of Fame Moment

PHIL (OR SHOULD WE SAY "FAIL") MICKELSON
AT THE '06 U.S. OPEN
MAMARONECK, NEW YORK—JUNE 18, 2006

Television commentator Johnny Miller summed it up best, watching Phil Mickelson spraying tee shots like a lawn sprinkler throughout the final round of the 2006 U.S. Open: "Ben Hogan is officially rolling over in his grave."

To his credit, although he managed to hit only two fairways all day and was hamstrung by a series of boneheaded shots, like a fairway wood from the tangled rough that was advanced little more than the length of his shadow, Phil "the thrill" managed to stay near the lead all day at punishing Winged Foot. He was on top after fanning a drive on 17, the ball nearly coming to rest in a garbage bag, but hit another Houdini, curved it onto the green, two-putted for par, and held a one-shot lead at the last. All he needed was par to win, bogey to slip into a next-day play-off. Then came disaster.

Mistake one: the misbehaving driver, given yet another chance, was the club of choice off the tee. The breeze was against, and he claimed his 4-wood wouldn't get him far enough down the fairway to easily reach the green. Where was the 3-wood, you ask? In the car trunk. Mistake two: after another wild slice, this one coming to rest next to a hospitality tent, he attempted to overcook a 3-iron around an impeding tree, trying for another miracle curveball to the green. Instead, the ball whapped the bark, coming to rest perhaps 30 yards from the disbelieving golfer. In full meltdown mode, he buried his next shot in a greenside bunker. Mick's a sand master, but not even Lawrence of Arabia could've gotten this shot anywhere near the cup, and his blast trundled past the hole and trickled into greenside rough. Two wick-whacks later, Phil had officially snatched defeat from the jaws of victory.

Why did he hit driver yet again? Why, when his wedge work is the envy of Tour pros the world over, didn't he play out safely away from the tree, and attempt to win the national championship by getting up-and-down from short range? Worst comes to worst, if he missed the ensuing par putt for the title, he would've had an 18-hole play-off the next day against a less experienced opponent. Only Faltering Phil and his

Dr. Freud know the answer to that one. But here's the sad irony: both the late Payne Stewart and David Toms, at the '99 U.S. Open and 2001 PGA Championship, respectively, used that exact strategy to beat Mickelson, the strategy he eschewed that fateful Father's Day evening. In other words, they weighed their options, chose to play the percentages, got the ball back in play, and let their wedges do the talking. And ultimately, the winning.

Before he holed his double bogey putt, the would-be champ was crouched on the green, head in hands, as his disbelieving legions turned tail for the exits. He might have been reading the line, but he was also probably remembering the words of Argentine great Roberto DiVicenzo, who uttered this immortal phrase after his notorious Masters scorecard gaffe back in '68: "What a stupid I am."

Afterword

The Ultimate Hacker's Humiliation

Had Dickens been a hacker, he might have said: It was the best of times, it was the worst of times, it was the goofiest of times.

I speak of my experiences at exquisite Pine Valley, the stick-and-ball Shangri-La in southern New Jersey considered by many to be the world's finest golf course.

What makes Pine Valley the pinnacle of the game? It's more than the course, an otherworldly combination of gorgeous and dangerous, where each hole burns a permanent imprint into the consciousness of all but the most scatterbrained golfer. The psychological demands of the layout are unending, as virtually every drive or approach shot requires a forced carry, however modest, over sand, scrub, and ominous vegetation. Perhaps because the golf itself is so relentless in intensity, the rest of the experience is so wonderfully agreeable. The caddies are absolute marvels, and are able to unearth balls in the undergrowth and read double-breaking putts with equal aplomb. The clubhouse is simple and unaffected, but drips with golf history. The showerheads are the size of Frisbees, the food is superb, the drinks are stiff, the beer ice cold, and the membership roster littered with names like "Palmer,"

"Player," "Fazio," and "Thomson." What more can one really ask for? Excuse me, for I digress.

To appreciate the absurdity of this tale, one must first understand the normal state of my golf game. It's best described as occasional flashes of reasonable competence interrupted by long stretches of sustained mediocrity. My résumé is as sparse as a rye grass fairway in mid-winter, and contains just one round at even par, two holes-in-one, and three-putt greens with sickening regularity.

It was a wholly unexpected and delightful shock then, not only to be invited to play this garden of Eden, a golf course I never thought I'd see in person, but to overcome four sixes, several doubles, no birdies, and a couple of those aforementioned three-putts during my inaugural round several years ago and post a score of 78.

My spiked feet were ten feet off the ground as we headed to the dining room for lunch while I contemplated the magnitude of the achievement. Common wisdom at Pine Valley states that no first-timer will tour the treacherously dazzling layout in less than 80 strokes, and somehow I defied the odds and my own inabilities to do just that. It remains my single proudest moment on the golf course, and I have the framed scorecard hanging in my office to commemorate it.

Fast forward to two years later. I'm making an encore appearance, this time as the guest of none other than the club's former president and chairman of the board, a member with more than 50 years of tenure. This round is the antithesis of the first, forgettable from a playing standpoint in every way, other than the day's last shot. Determined to overcome the weak fade that's left me short and right of virtually every green on the property, I overcompensated on the final approach, unleashing a vicious pull that veered 30 or more yards left of the target line. It went through the trees and into the tiny parking lot adjacent to the clubhouse, coming to rest only after detonating the rear window of a late-model Mercedes.

Don't expect me to hit a medium-sized green with a pitching wedge. But if you need someone wielding a fairway wood to smash a piece of tempered glass the size of a large breadbox from 200 yards away, then apparently I'm your man.

The shock and embarrassment were mitigated a bit by the odd physics of the incident. My wayward rocket somehow eluded the much taller SUV parked two feet away from the low-slung coupe, and, much like the notorious bullet that killed John F. Kennedy, mysteriously swooped down to the target in a flurry of flying glass.

The incredible irony of the whole thing was the identity of my victim. I was expecting to be castigated by a Pine Valley member: a captain of industry, international jet-setter, former amateur champion, or some combination of the three. Instead the car's owner turned out to be another guest at the club, the executive editor of a golf magazine that I was contributing to with some regularity. To his credit I never saw the slightest hint of a scowl, sigh, shrug, or head shake when he learned of my misdeed. However, when I introduced myself as someone who worked regularly for his magazine, he offered a hearty handshake while cheerfully replying, "Not anymore." Insurance information was exchanged, I tossed apologies like confetti—indiscriminately and in all directions—and we parted ways.

A few days later I was the guest of the professional at another superb club in the area, Metedeconk National in Jackson, New Jersey. I had apparently purged the troubling incident from my mind, the golf gods were smiling once again, and just as with my initial foray at Pine Valley several years earlier, I unexpectedly walked off the 18th green having taken less than 80 blows.

My Pine Valley host is a member here as well, and I would relish the chance to someday return to Metedeconk. I'd no doubt play with unbridled confidence given an encore presentation, and it would have little to do with how well I played or the numbers adding up on the scorecard. You see at Metedeconk, there's a shuttle waiting by the final green. The parking lot, chock full of shiny, late-model imports, is way over on the other side of the clubhouse, about five hundred yards away.

Contributor Biographies

BILLY ANDRADE (TEE-BOX TRIPPER)

Billy Andrade has won four events and some $12 million in a PGA Tour career that began in 1987. Just as importantly, along with fellow Rhode Islander Brad Faxon, he runs Billy Andrade/Brad Faxon Charities for Children, Inc., which was formed in 1991 and has raised more than $5 million for children in Rhode Island and southeastern Massachusetts.

BO BOWDEN (DISROBING FOR DOLLARS)

Like a Bronx-born kid who ends up playing for the Red Sox, Bo Bowden left Athens, Georgia (home of UGA) to play golf at rival Georgia Tech. He joined the PGA of America Apprentice Program in 1980, and has since held professional positions in Georgia, Florida, North Carolina, and South Carolina. In 2002 he initiated his current position as director of golf at the Reserve at Lake Keowee, a notable Jack Nicklaus design in the upstate region of South Carolina.

ALAN CARTER (RICK O'SHEA)

It's all in the family for Ontario native Alan Carter, who followed his golf course superintendent father into the business. He's been the director of golf at Jasper Park Lodge, one of Canada's most esteemed and revered courses, since 1994, and has been nominated as Alberta's Club Professional of the Year on three separate occasions. Alan has won numerous Pro-Am events, and has finished in the top 20 at the Canadian Club Professional Championship five times.

CHRIS CARTER (THE DINK)

Before taking his current position at The Hamlet Golf and Country Club on Long Island, Chris Carter learned the trade at some of the most prestigious golf enclaves in his native New York. He began his career in Florida, then went to the Midwest, apprenticing at storied Medinah in 1990, working the U.S. Open. He headed back toward the big city, and spent a decade in total at metropolitan mainstays Pelham Country Club and Meadow Brook Club, prior to landing the top spot at Hamlet in 2004.

DAVE CHRISTENSON (THE DOUBLE HITTER)

Dave captained the Washington State Cougars during his collegiate days and made it to the round of 16 at the 1990 USGA Public Links Championship. He spent a decade as an assistant professional at Indian Canyon Golf Course in Spokane, Washington, and then truly went Native American. He went east across the nearby Idaho border, and has been the director of golf at Circling Raven Golf Club since the day the course opened. Owned by the Coeur d'Alene tribe, Circling Raven has received numerous awards since its 2003 debut, and is already considered not only one of the premier courses in Idaho, but in the entire Northwest region.

BETH DANIEL (ANNA BANANA)

Once she was the Rookie of the Year, twice she was the U.S. Amateur Champion, and three times the Player of the Year on the LPGA Tour, so Beth Daniel has rarely had to yell "Fore!" With more than 30 official victories, including a Major at the LPGA Championship, it's no surprise that Beth is a member of both the World Golf and LPGA Halls of Fame.

NEEL DEROUEN (THE WORM BURNER)

Neel is a Class "A" professional and the director of golf at Gray Plantation in Lake Charles, Louisiana. The course is a charter member of Louisiana's award-winning Audubon Golf Trail, and considered among the top five courses in the state. It has also been named among the top 100 public courses in the United States.

MIKE DYNDA (EVEREST)

Mike is both the director of instruction at Blue Bell Country Club in Philadelphia and the men's golf coach at Drexel University. Since turning professional in 1987, he has earned 20 victories on the local professional circuits. He was named the Philadelphia PGA Teacher of the Year in 2005, and followed up that honor by coaching two different state open champions, in Pennsylvania and Delaware, in 2006.

FAITH EGLI (THE BUNKER BUMPER)

Faith is a former golfer at Michigan State University, where she was twice named to the All–Big Ten Team. The head golf professional at Congress Lake Club in Hartville, near Akron, she is the first-ever woman head pro at an Ohio private club. She has received the Lifetime Award of Merit from the Northern Ohio PGA, and was named one of the nation's top teachers by the Consumers' Research Council of America.

BRAD FAXON (ON IN TWO, OFF IN THREE)

Brad Faxon, an eight-time PGA Tour winner, is considered one of the premier putters of the modern era. He's made a million putts and some 18 million bucks, and has represented his country in the Walker Cup, Ryder Cup, and Dunhill Cup.

JOHN FERREBEE (THE BUNKER BLADER)

Originally from the Pocono Mountains of Pennsylvania, John Ferrebee came south to Hilton Head Island more than 30 years ago. He is the Director of Golf at the Daufuskie Island Resort and Breathe Spa, a charming 36-hole facility that's just a quick ferry ride away from Hilton Head. John has had the opportunity to work with some of the most recognized teachers in America through his affiliation with the *Golf Digest* Schools and the Troon Signature Golf Schools.

SEAN FISTER (SHORTY DRIVER)

Sean Fister is a three-time World Long Driving Champion, winning the titles in 1995, 2001, and 2005. The decade span between his first and most recent titles is the longest in LDA history.

BARRY FLEMING (THE BUNKER CHUNKER)

It's often said that a solid golf game can assist one's business career, and Barry Fleming is proof positive. He's been a PGA golf professional since 1975, played on Tour for a bit in the early '80s, and qualified for the '83 U.S. Open at venerable Oakmont. He's been the president of Club Key Golf Passbook since 1984, with 9,000 members and 500 affiliate courses. His other company, called Golf, Reservations & Events, Inc., currently operates pro-Am golf tournaments in Las Vegas and Cabo San Lucas, Mexico.

TERRY FLORENCE (SIDEWAYS)

Terry is the Grand Old Man of golf in Charleston, South Carolina, with 30-plus years in the business. He served as the director of golf at Wild Dunes Resort for more than 20 years. He has served in the same position at the remarkable Bulls Bay Golf Club since its 2001 debut. He is a two-time South Carolina Open Champion, a four-time South Carolina PGA Champion, and a recent inductee into the state's golf hall of fame.

Fred Funk (The Assassin)

One of the most precise drivers in golf history, "Fairway" Fred Funk has won the PGA Tour driving accuracy title seven times, finished in the top three more than a dozen times in total, and never been lower than seventh overall since 1991. He's also won eight Tour titles, including the ultra-prestigious Players Championship. He has well over 20 million reasons to believe that the Key Shot is the Tee Shot.

Douglas Goubault (Greta Garbo)

Canadian ex-pat Douglas Goubault is the first Director of Golf at the Mayakoba Resort's El Camaleon Golf Club, in Mexico's idyllic Riviera Maya. The stunning Greg Norman–designed golf course plays annual host to the first PGA Tour event ever held in Mexico—the Mayakoba Golf Classic, Riviera Maya–Cancun. Also an accomplished amateur player, Douglas captained Team Canada at the World University Championships in Northern Ireland in the year 2000.

Mike Harmon (Dr. Double Cross)

In 20-plus years as a Class "A" professional, Mike has won numerous awards, including the National PGA Merchandiser of the Year (Private category) in 2004 and the National PGA Bill Strausbaugh Award in 2006, presented to a pro who distinguishes himself through community service, and by mentoring fellow professionals in improving their employment situations. But this former PGA Tour player is best known as the original director of golf at Secession Golf Club in Beaufort, South Carolina, a walking-only, caddie-only facility that is one of the finest clubs in the nation.

MIKE HAYES (TEE-TOTALED)

A PGA Member since 1995, Mike Hayes has given instruction at over 200 corporate clinics. For nearly a decade he served as the head professional at Ford's Colony Country Club, in Williamsburg, Virginia, overseeing 54 holes of championship golf. Since 2003 he's been the head pro at the Rees Jones–designed Country Club of Hilton Head, located on the world-renowned barrier island off the South Carolina coast.

CHRIS MARTINEZ (MR. MUD)

Chris Martinez was born in Abilene and played for the University of Texas at Arlington. He credits two golf legends with reputations as big as the Lone Star State itself in shaping his instruction philosophy. He was a disciple of Byron Nelson and Hank Haney, working under and befriending them both. Now he's the director of golf at Querencia, a Tom Fazio dazzler in Cabo San Lucas, Mexico. He presides at the most exclusive private club on the Baja Peninsula, where an additional 18 holes will soon spring from an incredible desert landscape.

Dr. Doll Miller (Dyslexia)

Doll Miller is the head of refractive surgery at the Georgia Eye Institute, and has performed thousands of LASIK surgeries. Back in the Nixon years, she was the reigning National Girls' Junior Golf Champion and the New York Women's Amateur Champion concurrently.

Mike Mitchell (In Love with Loft)

Mike learned the value of loyalty from his grandfather, who spent nearly 50 years as the pro at Onondaga Country Club in upstate New York. Beginning as a 13-year-old caddie at Ridgemont Country Club in Rochester, Mike became their head professional at age 27, and remained in the position for two full decades. He was awarded an honorary life membership at the club when he left in 2005 to become director of golf at the ultra-posh Carnegie Abbey Club in Newport, Rhode Island.

Greg Norman (The Explosion Corrosion)

"The Great White Shark" is one of the most exciting golfers of the modern era. He amassed 20 PGA Tour titles, including two British Open Championships, and nearly 70 other international victories. He is an international developer of premier residential golf course communities, and his imprimatur is on wine, sportswear, turfgrass, event planning, and restaurants. He is especially in demand as a golf course designer. His design El Camaleón, located south of Cancun on the

Yucatan Peninsula, plays host to the Mayakoba Classic, which is the first PGA Tour event to ever be contested in Mexico.

Dave Pelz (The Pastor of Disaster)

This former NASA rocket scientist has spent most of his professional life proving that a solid short game isn't rocket science. It's just implementing the proper technique, playing the percentages, and practicing. Pelz is a best-selling author, television personality, speaker, and short-game-coach-to-the-stars, including Phil Mickelson, Vijay Singh, and Mike Weir. His latest book is *Dave Pelz's Damage Control*, which will help minimize disasters all over the course.

Reilley Rankin (The Root of all Evil)

Reilley is an up-and-comer on the LPGA Tour, where she's enjoyed fully exempt playing privileges and some $600,000 in earnings since her rookie season in 2004. She was a three-time All-American at the University of Georgia, but her golf career nearly ended in 1999 when a lakeside cliff-jumping accident resulted in a broken sternum and multiple back fractures. There were doubts whether she'd ever be able to walk, much less play competitive golf again. But her determination and resiliency led to a triumphant recovery, and after a years-long recuperation she helped lead Georgia to the 2001 NCAA Women's Golf Championship before embarking on her professional career.

ANDREW RICE
(RAPTURE ON THE RANGE, REMORSE ON THE COURSE)

Andrew is the director of instruction at Berkeley Hall, in Bluffton, South Carolina. He presides over a practice facility so comprehensive and cutting-edge that many experts consider it the finest in the world. He won three collegiate events while playing for the University of Central Florida. Though he originally hails from South Africa, he was still named as a second-team All American, and was a two-time Academic All-American besides. Prior to his arrival at Berkeley Hall, Andrew spent more than five years working as a senior instructor for renowned golf guru David Leadbetter.

LOREN ROBERTS (THE YIPPER)

This long-time PGA Tour and now Champions Tour star is a picture-book example of the old adage "drive for show and putt for dough." Roberts has more than 18 million reasons why aspiring golfers should put their time in on the putting green, not to mention eight PGA Tour titles, and five (and counting) victories, including two Majors, on the Over-50 Circuit.

CHARLIE RYMER (JACK THE PANTS RIPPER)

Charlie Rymer is a television personality who was a three-time South Carolina junior golf champion, a two-time All-American at Georgia Tech, and the 1985 USGA junior champion. His combined PGA and Nike Tour earnings were about $500,000, but his expenses were $700,000.

TAD SANDERS (CART-PATH BOUNCE)
This University of Virginia grad has one of the biggest jobs in golf—literally. Beginning as an assistant pro more than 20 years ago, Tad has risen through the ranks to become the director of golf at the expansive Landings Club in Savannah, Georgia. Tad oversees not one course or two, but six. Not one stand-alone pro shop, but four. Not a single head professional and a handful of assistants, but four and ten, respectively. And untold miles of cart paths. He's also served on the Georgia PGA Board of Directors and been lauded as Georgia's East Chapter Golf Professional of the Year.

J.J. SEHLKE (WRONG-BALL RALPH)
Although he's a bona fide PGA Professional and a former scholarship golfer at Western Kentucky and Miami, with a career-low round of 64, J.J. Sehlke has spent most of his career in upper management. He's held the general manager position at fine clubs and resorts throughout the Southeast. Currently he's the managing partner at Coral Ridge Country Club, a historic club in Fort Lauderdale that was founded by esteemed golf course architect Robert Trent Jones more than 50 years ago.

Bill Tooley (Uneven Steven)

Though he was born, raised, and began his golf career in neighboring New York state, Bill Tooley has found success in the Green Mountains of Vermont. A golf professional since 1989, he has been the head professional at Brattleboro Country Club since 2000. He was named the 2006 New England PGA Professional of the Year in the Vermont Chapter, and has been a two-time nominee for merchandiser of the year. Tooley has also served as the Vice President and Tournament Director of the Vermont chapter of the New England PGA and has been a Vermont PGA board member since 2001.

J.D. Turner (Pop-Up Boy)

PGA Master Professional J.D. Turner is one of the original members of *Golf Magazine's* Top 100 Instructors Panel. He spent 25 years in various head pro positions in his native Iowa, and is a five-time Iowa Open Champion. J.D. is now the principal of Turner Golf Group, specializing in corporate golf schools nationwide.

Ken Weyand (The Whiffer)

Born in Ohio, reared in California, with significant stretches in golf capitals like Hilton Head, Orlando, and Ponte Vedra Beach (Florida), Ken Weyand has chased the little white ball and held prestige positions from coast to coast. He's now the director of golf at Glenwild Golf Club in Park City, the top-ranked course in the state of Utah. The 15-year PGA pro is a national staff member with Titleist, where he has been a Certified Custom Club Fitter for more than a decade.

BOB WOLCOTT (WHEN IT'S BREEZY, SWING CHEESY)

Bob Wolcott was an All-SEC golfer and First Team All American while at the University of Georgia. He is the former state open champion of Tennessee, Arkansas, and Missouri, and a former Tennessee Amateur Champion. His PGA Tour career was highlighted by a pair of third-place finishes. Bob is currently the KemperSports General Manager and Director of Golf at Tunica National in Tunica, Mississippi, and has an ownership interest in GreyStone Golf Club in Dickson, Tennessee.

HEIDI WRIGHT (OFF-THE-PLANET JANET)

Heidi captained the golf team at Bowling Green State University her senior year, and learned her trade at storied Inverness Club in Toledo, Ohio. Just a month after she took the first assistant's position at Moss Creek in Bluffton, South Carolina, her new boss left for greener pastures. Heidi was named the head pro and has been running the show at this 36-hole Tom Fazio facility since 1994.

Jeff Yost (Aquaman)

Jeff Yost is the Head Golf Professional for the city of Charleston, South Carolina, and works at the Muni. Much like Heidi Wright, Jeff played on the Golf Team at Bowling Green State University in the late '80s. He started playing professionally in 1991, became a PGA Professional in 1997, and has worked with Aquamen from all over the United States. His experience in Northern California (cold water), Colorado (deep water), Florida (too many prehistoric critters to take undue risk), and South Carolina (see Florida) has helped many golfers lower their golf ball loss and dry cleaning bills.

Mike Zaranek (Woodrow Wilson)

Mike is the long-time head professional at the Crumpin-Fox Golf Club, a wonderful and woodsy retreat in Bernardston, Massachusetts. This top-notch facility is considered one of the finest courses in New England and among the nation's best public-access tracks. Mike was the western Massachusetts PGA Player of the Year in both 2005 and 2006.